A View from the Machan

How Science can Save the Fragile Predator

K. Ullas Karanth

Illustrated by
Maya Ramaswamy

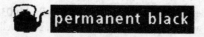

permanent black

Published by

PERMANENT BLACK
Editorial office: D-28, Oxford Apartments, 11 I.P. Extension,
Delhi 110092
and
'Himalayana', Mall Road
Ranikhet 263645

Distributed by

ORIENT LONGMAN PRIVATE LTD
Bangalore Bhopal Bhubaneshwar Chandigarh Chennai
Ernakulam Guwahati Hyderabad Jaipur Kolkata
Lucknow Mumbai New Delhi Patna

ISBN 81-7824-137-4

Typeset in Goudy by Eleven Arts, Delhi 110035
and printed and bound by Pauls Press, Okhla, New Delhi 110020

Dedicated to two great biologists who taught me
to think clearly about wildlife

Dr George B. Schaller

and

the late Dr John F. Eisenberg

Contents

Contents

Foreword

by George B. Schaller
Wildlife Conservation Society, New York

The tigress Sundari ambles to a pond, crouches to drink, then reclines with her hindquarters in the water. At the sound of a vehicle she retreats, her rust-gold coat blending into the pale yellow of bamboo as if she has never been. But a few minutes later she returns and halts by a tree only thirty meters from where Ullas Karanth and I sit motionless on the ground. Sundari sniffs the bark, rubs a cheek on it, and then swivels around to mark with a squirt of scent. It is mid-March 1991, and I am in India's Nagarahole National Park to learn from the long-term tiger study conducted here by Ullas and his co-workers. In Sundari's presence we do not dwell on the science of her behavior or on conservation. We are too enthralled by her elegance, restrained power, and sheer beauty. Indeed Sundari means 'beautiful.' Here is one of the most wonderful expressions of life on earth and it lifts our spirits.

In an age when nature is being viewed mainly in terms of natural resources, in dollar values, my heart speaks to Sundari. She is a strong reminder that conservation is also a moral issue of assuring other beings on this planet their right to exist. Fortunately religious belief and national pride have contributed to the tiger's survival in India and more remain in that country than any other. Nevertheless, on viewing a tiger I feel indignation that its survival is so wholly dependent on human whim. Respect for the environment, a loyalty to the earth, should be part of everyone's ethical attitude and responsibility, whether rich or poor, urban or rural, if we expect plants and animals to persist in all their variety and ecological complexity. The Hindu goddess Durga rides a tiger to defeat the evil that affects the world, including, I presume, the mindless destruction of our environment.

The tiger may be a natural icon of India, but it does kill livestock and occasionally people, transgressions for which it is trapped or poisoned. Gone from Turkey, Iran, and several other countries of its vast former range, its habitat fragmented, and ever larger forest tracts empty because of intensive poaching for its skin and bones, the tiger is in danger of vanishing from yet more countries. However, options remain even where the species is now rare. There is cause for optimism. Tigers are resilient, forest persists, and the animal has a worldwide constituency concerned about its fate. Conferences establish conservation goals, determined advocates promote action, and field biologists observe the tiger's habits, determine its status, and monitor populations. Yet far too few skilled investigators are active to study the tiger and its prey, train local staff to collect relevant information, and resolve conflicts between communities and wildlife. The status of tigers remains speculative in several countries, and we even have too little hard information from various parts of India.

Tiger conservation, as that of other species, has four cornerstones. First and most basic is knowledge of tiger ecology at each site, including information on prey species and the human population, upon which realistic and innovative conservation measures can be based. Conservation also depends on well-maintained and strictly protected reserves and other key areas with a guard force to deter poaching and degradation of the landscape by people and livestock. Solid domestic and international wildlife laws with vigorous enforcement against trade in tiger products are also essential. And, finally, local communities must be involved in the conservation effort through education and active participation, and a partnership with local government and other institutions must be initiated and maintained.

I mention these issues because no one in India or elsewhere in the world has done more to promote all aspects of tiger conservation than Ullas Karanth. With deep commitment, Ullas has spent a quarter century among tigers, becoming India's finest field biologist and the tiger's most persistent and successful advocate. His superb science has enhanced his role as conservationist. He has developed reliable techniques of censusing tigers and demonstrated the direct link between tiger and prey abundance. His depth of knowledge has influenced government policy and reserve management in India as well as perceptions and research techniques internationally. His writing, both scientific and popular, including such books as *Monitoring Tigers and their Prey* and *The Way of the Tiger*, have influenced a wide audience. Ullas has also trained a core of young field biologists whose dedication and enthusiasm impressed me greatly. Most recently Ullas has initiated a graduate program in conservation biology at a university in Bangalore. For decades to come the knowledge, inspiration, and devotion to wildlife and wilderness instilled by Ullas in others will continue to flow onward

and outward to help the tiger and other species endure. The articles collected in this volume are both a testament to and legacy of Ullas's concern and vision for India's wildlife.

Above all, Ullas is full of optimism. He is confident that the number of tigers can increase, given our will power, passion, perseverance, and ever-lasting commitment, and he knows that people, livestock, and tigers can coexist if properly managed. As Teilhard de Chardin wrote: 'The future belongs to those who give the next generation reason to hope.'

Acknowledgements

I have drawn on a great deal of my earlier writings for the essays in this book. I am grateful to the original publishers for allowing the use of this material. The relevant articles are listed below.

'Turning Natural History into Science: The NZP Nexus', *Zoogoer*, vol. 17 (2), March–April 1988, 8–10.

'Understanding Tigers', *Wildlife Conservation*, vol. 98 (3), May–June 1995, 26–37, 74.

'Wildlife Management: The Search for Auditors', *The Hindu Survey of the Environment* 1996, 145–51.

'Predators and Prey: Nature Strikes a Balance', National Council for Science and Technology Communication, Bombay National History Society, and *Sanctuary*, 1997, 1–64.

'Sacred Groves for the 21st Century', *Seminar* 466, June 1998, 25–31.

'Nagarahole: Shrine or Market in the Global Village?', in K.H. Redford (ed.), *Culturally Conflicting Views of Nature*, Conservation and Development Forum, University of Florida, 1999, 23–6.

'Here a deer . . . There an elephant!' *Wildlife Conservation*, vol. 102 (3), May–June 1999, 30–5.

'Wildlife: Protect Sanctuaries', *The Hindu Survey of the Environment* 2000, 77–84.

'Tigers go Wild', *Royal Wings*, September–October 2000, 30–3.

The essays in this collection result from my active engagement with wildlife issues for over three decades. Numerous individuals and institutions have been helpful to me in this process. Although it is impossible to acknowledge all of them here, I must try to mention at least some key names.

The Wildlife Conservation Society, New York has supported me professionally since 1988, giving me enviable freedom to combine my pursuit of wildlife science with the practice of conservation. The Save the Tiger Fund of the National Fish and Wildlife Foundation, Washington DC, the Division of International Conservation in the United States Fish and Wildlife Service, the 21st Century Tiger Consortium of Global Tiger Patrol, UK and the Zoological Society of London have also supported my work. I am grateful to all these institutions.

My father Shivarama Karanth and my favourite 'aunt' Dr Vasantha Sathyashankar encouraged my childhood interest in natural history. I am also grateful to S. Shyam Sundar and K.P. Achaiah who guided me into the jungles as a teenager, providing me with my first flesh-and-blood encounters with wildlife.

I am indebted to my naturalist friends who, over the years, have been an amazing source of strength, particularly K.M. Chinnappa, Radha Chinnappa, V. Krishna Prasad, Praveen Bhargav, D.V. Girish, Samba Kumar, Sanjay Gubbi, Vikram Nagaraj, Javaji Amarnath,

G.R. Sanath Kumar, Niren Jain, G.N. Ashoka Vardhana, Thamoo Pooviah, Satish Appachu, Shekar Dattatri, T.S. Gopal, Raj Nooyi, Jayaram Bhat, Nina Rao, Maya Ramaswamy, H.N.A. Prasad and Harsh and Poonam Dhanwatey. Their friendship and support have been crucial for my work.

My research work on wildlife has necessarily to be conducted in forest areas. Although the level of enthusiasm of the forest department for my work has usually waxed and waned in response to the exigencies of local conservation politics, several individual officers have been helpful at various times. While naming all of them here is impossible, I must at least acknowledge U.T. Alva, A.C. Lakshmana, S. Deb Roy, P.K. Sen, H.S. Panwar, S. Parameshwarappa, B. Majumdar, Kishore Rao, Vinod Rishi, Dipak Sarmah and C. Srinivasan. The list of forest rangers, foresters, guards, watchers and tribesmen who have sweated it out in the field with me is just too long to recount: but I acknowledge their contributions deeply.

Several other prominent conservationists have helped my work over the years. In this regard, I am grateful to Valmik Thapar, Brijendra Singh, Toby Sinclair, Mahendra Vyas, Belinda Wright, Bittu Sahgal, M.K. Ranjitsinh, Amanda Bright and Geoffrey and Diane Ward.

I owe intellectual debts to several teachers and professional colleagues who have generously shared their knowledge with me and encouraged my academic aspirations. A partial list of these individuals includes: George Schaller, John Eisenberg, Mel and Fiona Sunquist, Jim Nichols, John Seidensticker, John Robinson, Kent Redford, Alan Rabinowitz, Josh Ginsberg, Rudy Rudran, Jack Frazier, Chris Wemmer, M.D. Madhusudan, Raghu Chundawat,

Ajith Kumar, A.J.T. Johnsingh, Ravi Chellam, R. Sukumar and S.N. Hegde.

I am grateful to Anuradha Roy for her skilful editing, that improved this text greatly, and to Mahesh Rangarajan for sharing his valuable insights and commenting on earlier drafts.

My heartfelt thanks to my wife Prathibha who, despite her avowed lack of interest in natural history, has been a rock-steady source of support for three decades, and to my daughter Krithi who insists on admiring me greatly for no reason that I can discern.

K. ULLAS KARANTH

I

A View from the Machan

MY MEMORY DOES NOT GO BACK FAR enough to a time when I was not passionately interested in wild animals. They have always dominated my consciousness, taken over my other selves: the schoolboy growing up in a village in Karnataka; the college student, and, thereafter, the engineer in Bangalore and practising farmer near Nagarahole that I was for several years. Until 1984 it was a hobby. Then, abandoning my past lives, I embarked on a process of formally retraining myself as a wildlife biologist, a profession and a pleasure that has occupied me ever since.

There was not much I could do about my passion in school. Indian schools and universities have traditionally confined 'biology' within the four walls of a laboratory and valued the microscope more than the binocular. Most teachers of zoology in undergraduate colleges could not identify even common bird species around them. Educational and career opportunities were almost non-existent

for zoology students, unless they opted to become doctors, microbiologists or geneticists. Uninterested in such options, I became first an engineer, and later a farmer in careers that were successful materially, if not spiritually. All through this period, from the 1960s to 1980s, I continued to be a keen amateur naturalist, and involved myself in the nascent wildlife conservation movement in India. The writings of Indian conservation pioneers like E.P. Gee, M. Krishnan and Zafar Futehally greatly influenced me.

By 1983, I was in my mid-30s in a rut so comfortable, abandoning it was foolhardy. Yet wildlife continued to call out to me. I wanted to do wildlife work full time. I knew wildlife conservation could no longer be based merely on the natural history that Gee, Krishnan and Futehally talked about. Neither could it be rooted in a conveniently *laissez-faire* philosophy of doing nothing. Conservation could not continue as a spectator sport, based on sentiment and instinctive 'seat of the pants' reactions to emerging problems. Natural history had to transform itself into an applied science based on a solid foundation of modern wildlife biology. The Smithsonian Tiger Ecology Project, initiated a decade earlier in neighbouring Nepal, had already demonstrated the fruitfulness of such an approach to wildlife conservation. But the Indian educational system showed little sign of changing in order to provide the basis that conservation now clearly needed. There was no place in my own country where I could get the education I needed.

In December 1983, the Bombay Natural History Society, India's venerable conservation organization, hosted an international wildlife conference. As some of Asia's leading conservationists, Salim Ali of India, Boonsong Lekagul of Thailand and S. Dillon Ripley of the Smithsonian Institution in Washington DC, cogitated on stage, I searched out the three biologists who I knew had been involved

with the Nepal tiger study: Mel Sunquist, John Seidensticker and Dave Smith. It was tiger ecology that interested me most. All of them encouraged me and as a first step, introduced me to primate biologist Rasanayagam Rudran, who was part of the large Smithsonian–National Zoo contingent at the conference. I described to him the peculiar difficulties of an Indian engineer-turned-farmer who wanted to now turn wildlife biologist; Rudy (as Rudran insisted on being called) listened intently and then encouraged me to seek admission to the Wildlife Management Training Program that he was running at the National Zoo's Conservation and Research Center (CRC), at Front Royal, Virginia. I pleaded that I simply did not have, what was by my standard, the fortune required to cover the expenses involved. Rudy replied that while he could not supply me the merit every candidate needed for admission to the course, he would try to find the money to cover me if I made it through the selection process. Fortunately, I managed my side of it, the 'merit': I got a cable in March 1984, informing me that I had been selected for the course. Rudy, keeping his side of the bargain, assured me that the 'Friends of the National Zoo' would fund me. I was soon on my holy pilgrimage to the land of Aldo Leopold.

At that time, there were many Western zoos that cashed in on the attraction that exotic animals from developing countries held for the American public. Western biologists went to remote parts of the earth to study such animals and cover themselves in glory. There were, however, very few institutions that cared enough to help biologists and managers from these developing countries to do what mattered most: to stand on their own feet and manage their wildlife resources wisely in the difficult years to come. The Wildlife Management Training Program run by Rudy was probably the most effective and far-reaching of all such efforts at that time.

In the summer of 1984, I reached the Smithsonian's sprawling Conservation Research Centre nestling in the beautifully wooded Virginia countryside next to the Shenandoah National Park. We were thirteen trainees: three each from India and Sri Lanka, two from China and Malaysia, and a trainee each from Nigeria, Zambia, and Peru. The kinds of wildlife habitat in our native lands ranged from the rainforests of Malaysia to the African savannahs. The species that we hoped to study included the Indian tiger and the Andean Vicuna. Our backgrounds and cultures differed vastly. But two things united us: our involvement in wildlife conservation and the keenness to learn.

After we had come to grips with basic animal study techniques, Rudy split us up into four smaller groups. During the last two weeks of the course we carried out separate group projects to put to test the skills we had learnt. The take-home message from the project was simple: although the animal species we were studying at the Centre were new to us, when applied correctly, the skills we were learning would work equally well on the native species of animals that we would eventually deal with in our homelands.

Although a quiet, low-key personality, Rudy was a tough taskmaster. Originally from Sri Lanka, Rudy had got his doctorate working in Uganda under the supervision of the world famous mammalogist John Eisenberg. Jack Frazier, a herpetologist who had been a student of Nobel Laureate Niko Tinbergen at Oxford, assisted him. Rudy and Jack knew exactly the kind of training we really needed. They focused on the practicalities of wildlife study techniques, with precisely the 'hands-on' approach that was so sadly lacking in our home countries.

Up early in the morning, we slogged hard in the field, with a couple of intensive lecture sessions thrown in every day. In the classroom we were taught concepts that underlay various research techniques; then we rushed outdoors to practice what we had just been taught. No one could complain about the arduous fieldwork, because Rudy and Jack were out there working side by side with us.

The well-stocked scientific library and computer facilities at the CRC further expanded our intellectual horizons. After completing the training at Front Royal, I renewed contact with Mel Sunquist, who later became my graduate supervisor at the University of Florida.

During my professional career as a wildlife biologist, apart from my scientific publications, I wrote popular articles in my mother tongue, Kannada, as well as in English—a language I had learnt only in high school. These were published in various magazines or as booklets. This book contains eleven of my earlier essays, substantially revised, updated and often renamed. In addition, there are five new ones that I wrote specifically for this collection.

Most of us have an inborn fascination for wild animals; this is my belief. However, under the pressure of our Asian 'culture' that so centrally preoccupies itself with human affairs, this innate spark is effectively snuffed out through formal schooling and the burdens of daily life. The few who manage to keep the fascination for nature alive throughout their lives are the ones I call 'naturalists'—as opposed to 'environmentalists', 'activists' or even 'biologists', for whom conservation may just be another nine-to-five job. In 'The Spark of Natural History' (Chapter 2) I talk about early influences that helped to keep the spark of natural history alive inside me. This essay focuses on the naturalist and writer Kenneth Anderson who has inspired several generations of Indian naturalists with his colourful jungle tales.

Indian foresters, particularly those trench warriors who serve in the lower echelons of the service, played a central role in

recovering wildlife from the brink of virtual extirpation during the 1970s and 1980s. 'A Warrior in the Jungle' (Chapter 3) sketches the career of one such conservation stalwart, K.M. Chinnappa, whom I have known for over a quarter century. A humble forester, Chinnappa acquired great eminence in the conservation world because of his pioneering efforts to recover the wildlife in Nagarahole, which is now acknowledged to be one of the richest nature reserves in Asia.

Large predatory carnivores, such as tigers, leopards and dholes (Asiatic wild dogs), that thrive in Nagarahole, have enthralled me since my first visit to those jungles in 1967. My scientific study of these animals over the years could have turned into a tedious enterprise involving hard data collection and lots of 'grunt work'. But occasional high-voltage surges of excitement that course through me while watching these predators in action have turned tedium away. 'Nagarahole: A World of Predators' (Chapter 4) describes some exciting encounters with predators.

Old-style, 'qualitative' natural history has a tradition in India dating back three centuries, to native kings, Mughal emperors, and especially western naturalists. On the other hand, modern 'quantitative' wildlife biology is barely two decades old in India. Fortunately I have been able to channel my interest in natural history into modern wildlife biology, thus joining the ranks of pioneering Indian wildlife scientists like A.J.T. Johnsingh, Raman Sukumar, Ajith Kumar, Raghu Chundawat and Ravi Chellam. 'The Numbers Game' (Chapter 5) is about practising modern wildlife science. It reports on a successful conservation experiment involving the training of keen amateur naturalists to collect rigorous ecological data.

If there is one wild animal that has held me captivated throughout

my life, it is the tiger. 'Understanding Tigers' (Chapter 6) recounts how I employed techniques like radio-telemetry and other tools of modern wildlife biology to enter the secret world of tigers.

The next three essays on predators and predation comprise the theoretical core of this collection. They deal with the ecological and evolutionary realities that shape the life of predators, and explore how these factors affect our conservation efforts. 'Forces that Shape Predation' (Chapter 7) explains how predator ecology and behaviour have evolved in response to the forces of natural selection. 'Predation as a Way of Life' (Chapter 8) describes the ecology of predation. The article titled 'Predators and Humans' (Chapter 9) covers the critical issue of dealing with ecologically inevitable conflicts between large predators and human societies.

In the next two essays, I switch back to tigers again, and elaborate on the challenges of wildlife conservation in our crowded subcontinent using the charismatic big cat as an example. 'Can We Save the Tiger?' (Chapter 10) provides an overview of past efforts to save tigers and the future challenges that conservationists must squarely face if tigers are to survive this century and beyond.

The next essay, titled 'The Many Ways to Count a Cat' (Chapter 11) explores the interface between wildlife science and conservation practice. This essay shows why sound wildlife science practised by competent wildlife biologists should be an essential ingredient of effective conservation. It also questions the present unscientific approach to wildlife management in India.

Protected areas in India were originally designated primarily for wildlife conservation. In the last two decades, however, they have come under attack as elitist irrelevancies. Consequently the rationale for securing them is increasingly being pushed backstage by the currently dominant, 'user-friendly' conservation paradigms.

The last two essays examine this issue. They argue for re-establishing the central role of effectively protected nature reserves in efforts to save global biodiversity. 'Sacred Groves for the New Century' (Chapter 12) provides the ecological justification for protecting nature reserves. This essay is a critique of the conservation paradigm of 'sustainable use as the sole key' to wildlife conservation. It suggests an alternative strategy based on the concept of 'Sustainable Landscapes' advanced by ecologist John Robinson. The last essay, 'Nagarahole: Shop or Shrine?' (Chapter 13), is a case study of how an effectively protected nature reserve can recover and protect fragile forms of biodiversity in the context of advancing development.

My view is an unapologetically bio-centric one: I am deeply concerned that wildlife and wild lands, which have evolved over millions of years must survive on this planet at least in their present remnant form. I believe that the present generation of humans has no moral right to extirpate wild nature, and that we hold nature in trust for future generations. More pragmatically, science now warns us that it would be decidedly unwise for mankind to pursue its reckless course of destroying nature, even for its own good. I hope this collection of essays advances both the above arguments with sufficient clarity and urgency.

2
The Spark of Natural History

I OFTEN ASK MYSELF WHAT MADE ME A naturalist. By the term 'naturalist' I don't mean someone who is formally trained in natural history. My idea of a naturalist is simply someone who loves to observe wild creatures, never tiring of it. A great many people can admire the grandeur of the Himalayan landscape, the beauty of the Taj Mahal or the brilliance of a ballet performance. However, the same people would be bored to tears at the very idea of sitting in a hide for hours—or trudging through miles of difficult jungle—in the mere hope of catching a fleeting glimpse of some wild creature. This focused fascination for 'living nature'—animals and plants—sets apart naturalists from aesthetes of other kinds.

I believe most of us are 'genetically programmed' to be fascinated by the animals around us, at least when we are very young. That is why children love pets, animal-toys, and visits to the zoo. However, as we grow older, this instinctive curiosity about nature rapidly

atrophies. The process of formal schooling compels us to focus our energies exclusively on human culture. Education makes us illiterates incapable of browsing through the magnificent library of nature. Naturalists survive this process of intellectual attrition usually because someone around them keeps alive their spark of natural history. In my own life, I have been fortunate in having several such people around me.

Typically, Asian cultures are uninterested in natural history. The average Indian is far less interested in natural history compared to his or her counterpart in the West. Even our noted writers, poets and journalists show scant regard for biological accuracy when they write about animals or birds. Fortunately for me, my father, the well-known Kannada writer, Shivarama Karanth, was an exception to this rule. He was deeply interested in the natural world. Set in the rural landscape between the Western Ghats and the coast of Karnataka, our home was abundantly stocked with natural history books and stacks of *National Geographic* magazines. I recall my father reading me Jim Corbett's *Man-eaters of Kumaon*, translating its fine prose—on the go—into Kannada. I must have been around eight, and could not understand a word of English. Around the same time, the mid-1950s, a favourite aunt of mine gave me her well-thumbed copy of Salim Ali's *Book of Indian Birds*. Despite its dreadful illustrations, the first edition of this classic guide launched my formal bird-watching career, when I used it to identify my first wild bird, a common tree pie.

Because of my father's deep distrust of any kind of formal schooling, I had all the time to wander in the woods around our home, watching birds all day. I eventually joined the sixth grade directly at high school, at the ripe old age of eleven.

In the mid-1960s, two remarkable men from the forest

department kept the fire of natural history burning in me. Ironically, these men were from the two extremes of this department's rigid hierarchy. At the lower end of the totem pole was a deputy ranger named K.M. Chinnappa who I met in Nagarahole (more about him in the next essay). At the top end was my cousin S. Shyam Sundar, a senior officer of the Indian Forest Service.

I got my first real wildlife watching experience with Shyam Sundar, sitting on a machan in the Shettihally forests of Shimoga observing half a dozen wary gaur at a salt lick. The brilliance of that moonlit night and the ghostly forms of the massive wild cattle are still vivid in my memory. Although Shyam Sundar was not a 'naturalist' by any means, he cared passionately for the forests and for the rule of the law. Despite the weaknesses in the prevalent game protection laws, he had begun to implement them in his forest jurisdiction, even while many of his own peers flouted them openly.

Shyam Sundar remains a knowledgeable forester, with a deep commitment to his profession. An upright and efficient officer, he towered over most of his colleagues both morally and intellectually. Because of his stature, commitment and persistence he was able to initiate many progressive forest conservation measures in Karnataka. His deep insights into the social realities of forest conservation in India significantly influenced me.

After learning to read English at high school, I came across Kenneth Anderson's books on man-eating tigers and leopards. His writings belonged to the genre of shikar tales that many white hunters of the Raj in India told. Anderson had me in his grip from the word go: I was almost like a helpless human victim in the jaws of one of his dreaded man-eaters.

Most of Kenneth Anderson's shikar tales are first-person narratives. His six books encompass a corpus of 52 stand-alone accounts. Many of them are tales of man-eating tigers and leopards that the author claims to have killed. Tales of these dreaded predators—labelled with chilling names, such as the 'Marauder of Kempakerai', 'Evil One of Umbalmeru', 'Bellundur Ogre' and the 'Assassin of Diguvametta'—are, without exception, feverishly gripping. Typically, each account contains vivid descriptions of the landscape, people and wildlife, followed by the details of a frustrating chase after the elusive, dangerous quarry, hair-raising initial encounters that result in lucky escapes for the author. And, a magnificent finale, in which Anderson delivers the *coup de grace* to the dreaded man-eater.

Not all of Anderson's stories are about man-eaters, however. He has also written about hunting ordinary tigers, leopards, elephants, and other big game. Some accounts describe less spectacular, but equally interesting, animals like sloth bears, wild dogs, hyenas, and jackals that the Anderson family often kept as pets. Anderson also talked about other animals like the four-horned antelope, ratel, or pangolin that were of little interest to most big game hunters of his day. Some of Anderson's narratives are simply about the joys of camping in the jungles, fundamentals of field craft, and about tracking wild animals by day or by night. A few stories are about encounters with an assortment of quaint, weird, and interesting people, ranging from artless tribal people to pompous officials. The chief ingredients in all these stories are: vivid natural history descriptions, exciting adventure and a hefty dose of 'jungle sociology'. These make a cocktail that is truly addictive.

Anderson's gift for evoking the jungle can be matched by few naturalist-writers. Whether he is describing a jungle sunset, a moonlit bamboo forest, the roosting call of the peafowl, alarm call of the deer, or the roar of a tiger, I almost felt, heard, saw, what he wrote. Here goes one such description:

It was late October. The worst of the monsoon had passed and storm-tossed rain laden clouds from the southwest no longer scudded across the sky to deluge the jungle with torrential showers . . . Multi-coloured orchids, dull green beard-like moss and the drab, grey lichen that mantled the erstwhile bare rocks, all looked fresh and clean.

The jungle tales of this Bangalore-based hunter were set in many wild places in a wonderful faunal region that stretches all the way between Kodagu (Coorg) in the west to Nandyal in the east; Salem in the south to Chitradurga in the north. Entertainment apart, the tales are of great value to present-day biologists assessing the decline of forests and wildlife in this region. There are no tigers in Tumkur district now, nor are there leopards within Bangalore city. The foothills of the Nilgiris and the forests of Shimoga that teemed with wildlife in Anderson's times have had a great wave of human-induced destruction sweep through them.

In terms of biological accuracy, Anderson's accounts of animal species are comparable to those of other colonial hunters of his era. His observations on animal tracks, calls, and hunting techniques reveal his deep field skills. Reading these books as a trained wildlife biologist, however, I now find that, like other hunters of his times, some of Anderson's natural history conjectures are untenable. However, as a schoolboy of fifteen, I was totally taken in by everything he said.

These books are also great fun to read because of Anderson's wonderful sense of humour, its Scottish character flourishing on Indian soil despite Anderson being a sixth-generation Scot in India.

Not for him the stiff upper lip or the starched collar of the typical sahib. Nor for him the straitlaced gentlemanly narrative of a Jim Corbett. To illustrate this point, I cannot resist citing a delightful account of how Anderson refused to vacate a forest rest house for the mighty District Collector himself, hanging pugnaciously on to 'his half' of the bungalow:

At about eight o'clock I saw a marvellous sight. The table had been laid for the great man's meal on the other half of the veranda by his *chaprasis* . . . There was snowy table linen, sparkling cutlery and crockery, and a cut-glass vase crammed with flowers . . . Then, the Collector came for dinner. Believe it or not, in spite of the sweltering heat, he wore a dress suit, complete with boiled shirt, bow tie and all! . . . I put on my oldest and most ragged khaki shirt and torn pants and squatted on the floor of the veranda at the other end, munching my dry *chapatties*. The Collector, sitting in solitary splendour, looked at me briefly and just once. He saw something that the cat must have left on the door step the night before, for he never looked up again.

Having got to know the irascible Anderson well, albeit many years after this incident, I have absolutely no doubt that every word above is true.

As a callow youngster I found Anderson's books even more enjoyable than those of my earlier hero, Jim Corbett. Anderson's south Indian locales, plants and animals were more familiar, and hence, personally more real to me than Corbett's world in the distant Himalayan foothills. Apart from which, there was plenty more action, thrill, humour and variety in the fare that Anderson served.

In 1971, after completing my engineering degree I moved to Bangalore to take my first real—and dreadfully boring—factory job. One of my first acts of escape was to trace my boyhood hero

Kenneth Anderson to his ramshackle house in White Field, a
Bangalore suburb. There he was in real life, a strong man, perhaps
in his late sixties, all too faithful to the self-portrait in his books:
right down to the scruffy khakis, ragged thick beard, and the
mischievous twinkle in pale blue eyes. His weedy garden was deep-
littered with dirt and dog turds. It sheltered several mongooses,
snakes and other assorted pets. I found Anderson did not live any
more with his wife Betty whom I had read about in his books.
Instead his companion was a charming Anglo-Indian lady much
younger than him, who I presumed was his second wife.

Anderson's passion for wildlife was undimmed too, and, as we
talked late into the evening about animals and jungles of southern
India, despite an age gap of more than forty years, and the deep
differences in our social backgrounds, we became good friends.
Anderson was every inch the tough jungle man and the incredibly
witty raconteur with a devil-may-care attitude that I had expected.
Presumably he took a liking to me because he spotted that spark
that burns inside all naturalists.

We met several times over the next few months, and whenever
Anderson came to the city on his rickety motorcycle, he dropped
in for a cup of tea at my sister's place in Richmond Road where I
stayed. We talked and talked about nothing but wildlife. Once I
even managed to cajole my brother-in-law to lend me his car so
that Anderson and I could make a field trip to his camp at the foot
of the Nilgiri hills. His fabled Mavanahalla camp turned out to be
just a mud hut. We wandered in the surrounding forests for a couple
of days, subsisting primarily on salty slices of smoked beef rolled
up in dry chapattis. Anderson seemed to carry an endless supply of
both these staples, which had obviously seen better days. We drank
muddy water from jungle streams and tried to track wild animal

spoor. But there was little wildlife to be seen, with the jungles overrun by village cattle and poachers.

Anderson bemoaned the fate suffered by these forests and wildlife at the hands of the 'local races' who it seemed to him were clearly unfit to govern themselves. I tried to cheer him up with the story of a wildlife recovery I had just begun to witness in the Nagarahole jungles to the west. We made a pact to visit Nagarahole next.

A few days later I heard Anderson was in hospital. When I visited, he held my hand and started talking excitedly about the details of our proposed trip to Nagarahole. His blue eyes twinkled at the prospect of seeing 'sloth bear cubs riding piggy-back on their mother'. I assured him, somewhat rashly, that all arrangements, including the aforesaid bears, were in place and we could visit Nagarahole as soon as he got out of hospital. That, however, was not to be. When I came out into the corridor, his lady companion who had been silent hitherto, hugged me and began sobbing. It turned out that Kenneth Anderson was terminally ill. He passed away a few days later.

Anderson's narrative skill almost convinces the reader that he was indeed the slayer of all those dreaded man-eaters. Yet, the sense of stark realism that Jim Corbett conveys in his man-eater stories through his spare prose and unvarnished attention to detail is missing here. So too are the dates that could help us fix a time-frame around the man-eating sprees of Anderson's big cats. Those of Anderson's contemporaries that I know, like the famous taxidermist Joubert Van Ingen of Mysore, are sceptical of the existence of these man-eaters. This difficulty in separating fact from fiction in Anderson's tales gets even more complicated as we read his accounts of black magic, sorcery, and evil spirits—and yes, even a sadhu who apparently could turn himself into a tiger.

There is no doubt that Anderson did shoot a few tigers and leopards. But his heart really seemed to be more in soaking up the jungle atmosphere and telling us all about it. His words somehow inject into our veins the same adrenalin that courses through his when he is out there tracking a tiger. Perhaps 'man-eaters' simply made his storytelling a little easier. I believe we should savour Anderson's writing just as we would enjoy a Steven Spielberg movie: by suspending disbelief. Surely one does not pass up a sumptuous Indian meal just because the masala is a trifle too rich?

Thirty years after Kenneth Anderson's death, I am glad to see his magic world of tigers, jungles and sorcerers lives on. His books are still being widely read not only in English, but ironically, also translated into my 'native' Kannada tongue that Anderson himself did not care much about! When I asked him why he did not speak the language, he told me that 'unlike the Tamils, the Canarese are not a sufficiently respectful race'—presumably to *Dorais* like Anderson himself. I am gratified that even in his death, my old friend continues to keep alive the spark of natural history alight among his numerous readers, respectful or otherwise.

3
A Warrior in the Jungle

NAGARAHOLE NATIONAL PARK, WHERE I have studied of tigers and other wildlife for the past two decades, stretches from the foothills of the Western Ghats into the Deccan plateau. The park covers an area of 640 square kilometres of beautiful forests in the districts of Kodagu and Mysore in Karnataka. This is a region where hunting is a deeply held tradition: the royalty of Mysore and their courtiers, Kodava warriors of Kodagu, and the native tribesmen of the Jenu Kuruba, Betta Kuruba and Yerava groups, have all hunted wildlife here over centuries. By the 1960s, hunting had almost wiped out tigers and other big game. Although technically illegal, such hunting enjoyed wide social acceptability. Under the weak game protection laws then in operation, practically no one was deterred from poaching.

When I visited Nagarahole for the first time in 1967, a genial, well-built man sporting close-cropped silver hair was the 'game ranger' there. K.P. Achaiah was a grizzled veteran of jungle warfare

from Lord Mountbatten's Burma campaign. When the Second World War ended, Achaiah had joined the forest department as a deputy ranger, and later risen up to the rank of a ranger, the highest he would ever go in the hierarchy. The sight of a scruffy teenager on a motorbike, who had come to 'watch animals'—instead of shooting them, as his peers were inclined to—must have piqued Achaiah's curiosity. He let me stay with him, took me for long walks in the jungle, and even plied me liberally with the potent Bison brand arrack that he favoured at sunset.

Achaiah was an expert elephant-catcher: he was reputed to have caught hundreds of wild elephants in the forests of Nagarahole. And he had achieved this safely and humanely, one animal at a time, using the 'pit method' traditionally used in Kodagu. He proudly contrasted his humane method of elephant capture with the cruelty and brutality of the more famous Mysore khedda that involved chasing, herding and corralling hundreds of wild elephants simultaneously.

Achaiah had a native genius in the business of caring for elephants and loved these animals with a rare passion. Although he had grown up in a local village, shot a tiger as a teenager, and lived in these jungle for very long, Achaiah's knowledge of natural history was based largely on what he heard from the Jenu Kuruba tribal people who lived around him. Consequently, it was a curious blend of ecological facts and fanciful myths.

His duty of trying to enforce the weak wildlife protection laws was a deeply frustrating one for Achaiah. In this land, and among his people, the right to hunt wild animals was a deeply held tradition. It was also a lucrative source of commerce. Achaiah would often tell me that his only hope of securing the future of Nagarahole lay in a young deputy ranger named Chinnappa who was assigned to logging duties in the park. 'Only if that tough youngster is made my deputy and follows my footsteps, these animals will be saved after my time,' he insisted. But such an event was as likely to transpire as a miracle, he rued, because senior officials posted such competent men only to the profit-generating logging duties. Usually only aged, infirm or otherwise incompetent men were assigned to game preservation duties.

However, two years later, thanks to the foresight of a senior officer named Ramachandra Chetty, such a miracle did manifest itself: Chinnappa was posted as Achaiah's deputy.

Although Chinnappa was eight years older than me, we were bound by the common passion for 'watching animals' rather than hunting them. We became friends almost instantly. We belonged to the new generation of Indian wildlife conservationists who did not have any roots in the hunting tradition. My love for wildlife could be explained to a certain extent by my middle-class upbringing and education. But Chinnappa came from a rural community of avid hunters. Strangely, he had never cared for that sport and had grown up with a deep love for animals. Unlike his fellow Kodava men, Chinnappa never ate game meat.

Our view of conservation differed sharply from that of other Indian hunter-naturalists, who even as late as the 1960s killed 'game for sport'. Some of them did so in the naïve belief that somehow they could keep out the 'destructive native poacher' through this process, while others simply could not give up the urge to hunt. Chinnappa had realized that the colonial rules of game quotas, which restricted hunting to the upper social classes, simply would not work in independent India. What was required was total protection for wildlife from all hunters, rich and poor alike.

Chinnappa was born and raised in a village on the edge of

Nagarahole and had been forced to seek a job without ever getting a chance to acquire a college degree. Yet his intellectual depth dwarfed that of his peers whose knowledge of natural history was largely based on hearsay. For example, although the local tribesmen were excellent trackers, they believed that wild dogs blinded their prey by sprinkling urine into its eyes. A senior forest official, who had shot several tigers during a career spanning four decades in the Nagarahole jungles, did not know what a four-horned antelope was, or that it actually occurred in his forests.

In contrast, Chinnappa updated his field knowledge by reading scientific books and tried to validate factoids of native natural history through personal observations. In practising this philosophy of constantly pitting abstract ideas against real world data, Chinnappa was the quintessential modern ecologist.

I possessed only the natural history knowledge that I gleaned from books. I had little experience of field craft or animal tracking. Chinnappa taught me skills that enabled me to read animal stories written into dusty forest trails. In turn, I supplied Chinnappa with wildlife books and initiated him into birdwatching, a science at which he became proficient quickly.

Taking a walk with Chinnappa through Nagarahole forests on pitch dark nights—equipped with nothing more than a little flashlight which he kept switched off most of the time—was a special thrill for me. These forests teemed with elephants and other potential dangers. However, Chinnappa could, seemingly miraculously, detect and avoid elephant herds in total darkness. He relied on subtle signals that I could not detect at all: the crackling of a twig, the rustle of dry leaves, the flapping of ears or the low rumble of an elephant tummy. The skill with which he negotiated the forests in darkness never ceased to amaze me. Chinnappa told me that early on he had worked hard to develop this skill, in order to ambush poachers who kept their flashlights switched on all the time.

Similarly, Chinnappa's skill in tracking spoor enabled him to follow elephant herds for hours on end, day after day, on foot. Such tracking made him understand the nuances of Asian elephant behaviour better than even formally trained elephant ecologists.

His forensic skills when examining the site of a tiger's kill, and analytically reconstructing details of the predatory act, were quite extraordinary. Chinnappa's ability to make accurate field observations quickly and reconstruct what happened were comparable to those of the best aboriginal trackers. I have no doubt in my mind that if Chinnappa had had the opportunity to be trained formally as a wildlife biologist, he would have ranked right up there with the likes of George Schaller, Ian Douglas Hamilton or Jane Goodall. Yet, here he was in Nagarahole: a humble cog in the massive machinery of the forest department.

My thirty-five years of friendship with Chinnappa not only taught me natural history field skills, they also gave me a unique ringside view of the battles to save nature in India. My friendship also provided me with a window into the personal triumphs and tragedies of a remarkable front-line warrior engaged in this battle.

I was not part of the forest service, which is the custodian of India's wildlife. I have, however, had the privilege (and I might add, the pain too) of associating closely with many forest officials for over three decades. With a few exceptions, the typical Indian forester's knowledge of wildlife ecology tends to be rather poor. This is because their primary source of information on wildlife does not come from formal training in wildlife biology or from scientific materials or even from direct personal observations. The primary source of such knowledge is often the jungle lore they hear from colleagues, subordinate staff, villagers or tribesmen. Given this, Chinnappa's exceptional natural history knowledge often led to great discomfiture among his superiors in the forest department. In a highly hierarchical, protocol-conscious department such bluntness was usually equated with unpardonable arrogance.

The 1960s were bad times for Nagarahole. Strong wildlife protection laws did not exist. People moved around the reserve with unrestricted abandon, encroaching productive habitats for agriculture, raising livestock and collecting forest products. Poachers of all sorts swarmed everywhere: the landowning classes used shotguns, tribal people employed snares, and livestock herders used poisons to destroy wildlife. The forest department concentrated its attention almost exclusively on logging, clear-cutting huge swathes of mixed natural jungles to replace them with monocultures of teak. For two decades, Chinnappa was a one-man army against all these forces of destruction. In the process, he became a hated enemy of many who wanted to use, misuse and abuse nature in Nagarahole.

In the 1970s, prospects for wildlife conservation took a dramatic turn for the better. Tough new wildlife laws were enacted, and even more surprisingly, they were implemented on the ground, at least in the newly created wildlife reserves.

Several social factors underlay this conservation revolution of sorts: a vocal middle-class constituency that emerged to support wildlife protection because of the awareness created by pioneers like E.P. Gee, Salim Ali, M. Krishnan and Zafar Futehally in the preceding decade. Prime Minister Indira Gandhi responded effectively to the concerns of this constituency, by not only enacting tough new wildlife laws, but also by exercising strong pressure on state governments—most under her own iron-handed rule—to ensure implementation of the new laws.

The forest departments of the states, despite their many failings, did respond by implementing the new wildlife protection laws effectively, if somewhat erratically. As illegal hunters, cattle herders, encroachers and forest product collectors were curbed, wildlife populations recovered. No doubt such recoveries were largely restricted to wildlife reserves in those state forests that were under government control. (Nothing changed, for example, in the north-eastern hill states where local communities controlled most wild lands.) Reserves that are known today for their abundant wildlife, such as Kanha, Corbett, Ranthambhore, Bandipur and Nagarahole, were all recovered from the brink of destruction during the 1970s.

The forest staff had to face the wrath of everyone who lost out because of the new curbs imposed on forest use. Chinnappa exemplified the finest elements among these trench warriors who recovered India's wildlife from virtual extirpation during the 1970s and 1980s. The wisdom of the senior officials, who kept him posted in Nagarahole through this decade, ensured that the experiment did not collapse midway. Inspired by Chinnappa's dedication many of his peers tried to follow his example. But few could stay the course like he did for three decades, against all odds.

Chinnappa's was a hard act to follow. In a department where siphoning off funds from 'works' (a euphemism for non-protective tasks such as civil construction and raising nurseries, planting and so on) was the norm, he took no cuts. Where other colleagues pleaded with their bosses for a larger share of the financial cake during the 'Annual Plan of Operations' exercises, Chinnappa took only what was needed. His wildlife management interventions were limited largely to protective duties, and driven solely by his ecological understanding of wildlife needs.

While his colleagues secured their financial futures, during his three-decade-long career in the forest department, Chinnappa had no time even to care for the five-acre coffee farm that he inherited, although it was right outside Nagarahole. The burden of maintaining the farm fell on his wife Radha. This courageous woman, trained by Chinnappa to be an expert shooter soon after they got married in 1969, braved the dangers of staying with him deep inside a jungle infested with thugs and criminals of all sorts. Radha visited the family farm whenever she could, and managed to keep it in good repair with the sweat of her brow. To this day, this small farm is Chinnappa's sole source of livelihood and security.

In the mid-1980s when I began my predator research project in Nagarahole as a graduate student at the University of Florida, Chinnappa and I were able to soak ourselves in the joys of modern field biology. We spent hours walking the forest trails to count prey species; collected predator scats and kills and finally captured and radio-tracked several tigers and leopards for the first time in India. Reputed wildlife biologists who visited my project, George Schaller, Mel Sunquist, John Seidensticker and Tom Struhsaker, were all impressed greatly by Chinnappa's zeal and field craft. Over the years, Chinnappa won many laurels for his conservation work: the Karnataka Chief Minister's Gold Medal in 1983 and the Wildlife Conservation Society's recognition in1988. Naturalist-writer Fiona Sunquist featured his profile internationally in an article titled 'Walking tall, talking tough' published in the *Wildlife Conservation* magazine. Historian Geoffrey Ward documented Chinnappa's achievements in his book *Tiger Wallahs*.

Ironically, although wildlife conservationists from far and wide recognized his accomplishments, Chinnappa continued to be feared and disliked by many of his local neighbours. To illegal hunters, timber smugglers, cattle herders and squatters he was, as ever, anathema.

People who lived around Nagarahole thought Chinnappa was an odd recluse: unlike other men of his caste, he did not eat any meat, let alone the game meat many liked; he rarely attended rituals like weddings and death ceremonies that traditionally bound people in his community. Chinnappa even prevented tourists in Nagarahole from 'having fun' by littering the park and disturbing animals. He would not fawn over local dignitaries and politicians when they came to visit. The majority of local people thought he was an upright but harsh man. The tribal people living in Nagarahole believed that he had magical powers over elephants, because he wandered alone at night!

I recall a visitor—who happened to be a relative of the forest minister at the time—complaining about being served 'ordinary food' at Nagarahole, not befitting his status. Chinnappa's retort was blunt and direct: 'This is the jungle. You should come here to watch animals, not to gorge yourself on fancy food. If you want better food, ask your exalted relatives to cook it for you next time.' On another occasion, Chinnappa rudely ticked off a senior police official who hinted at his preference for curry made from wild fowl instead of a domestic chicken.

All through his years in Nagarahole (1970–92), Chinnappa continued to have conflicts with local people who had interests in the forest: poachers, forest product smugglers and cattle grazers. Matters came to a head in 1988, when I was away at the University of Florida. One of Chinnappa's guards publicly shot a local coffee planter in broad daylight over a private quarrel: the victim had earlier killed and eaten a pet sambar deer that belonged to the guard. Local poachers and their political backers immediately

instigated a public agitation accusing Chinnappa of masterminding the murder. Under political pressure, Chinnappa was arrested and denied bail for a week. Although he was subsequently cleared of all blame in an enquiry, his enemies got him transferred out of Nagarahole. However, within a year, some of us conservationists lobbied hard and managed to bring him back to resume his vigil. He was again transferred out of Nagarahole under political pressure in 1990 only to be brought back a few months later as the park's protection nose-dived.

Finally, following the mysterious shooting of a poacher in the forests of Nagarahole in February 1992, local politicians engineered a major riot against Chinnappa. A frenzied, armed mob of about three hundred people invaded Nagarahole, ransacked buildings, burnt vehicles and assaulted forest staff. When the armed riot police on hand remained mute spectators under local political pressure, the mob went berserk and set fire to the forests using gasoline spray. In the summer heat, the flames spread and scorched about twenty square kilometres of forests. Not content merely with this, they went on to Chinnappa's village outside the park and burnt down his home.

Alerted by a friend, Chinnappa and Radha escaped in time to reach my home in Mysore. A network of young wildlife enthusiasts, which both of us had jointly built up over the years, now rallied to Chinnappa's defence. The scandalous riot and arson incident resulted in a strong reaction from the state government, which arrested the rioters and ordered a police enquiry that eventually cleared Chinnappa of any involvement in the murder of the poacher.

Although order returned to Nagarahole swiftly following the strong crackdown, Chinnappa and I realized that he could work there only at the cost of his own life. Chinnappa decided to retire from the forest service five years before his time, refusing all entreaties from his superiors to ask for a safe, 'lucrative' posting of his choice.

Why did the local thugs who rioted hate Chinnappa so strongly? This was not what occupied us. Why did the general public, who had no major conflicts with Chinnappa, not recognize and support his decades of service in Nagarahole? I reasoned with Chinnappa that the future of Nagarahole could be secured only if we could erase this apathy—which the miscreants had exploited—among local people. Law enforcement from within had to continue of course, but it was becoming untenable in the absence of a broader public acceptance and support.

In 1993, with support from the New York-based Wildlife Conservation Society and Global Tiger Patrol of London, Chinnappa started the Nagarahole Wildlife Conservation Education Project reaching out to the local students, youth and the public, relying on slide talks and field trips to enlist their support. Quite characteristically, Chinnappa refused to draw any salary from the donors, saying simply that the government pension and his farm met all his needs.

Equally characteristically, his conservation message to his audiences was strong and straightforward: 'Look how beautiful these animals are . . . do you know how useful they are to us? Saving wildlife is therefore both a practical and a moral imperative. Don't blame the government for everything or expect government officials to save this wildlife for you.' Then came the punchline 'All of us are a part of this problem, so we have to be part of the solution.'

A decade into its existence now, the direct message from the Nagarahole Wildlife Conservation Education Project has reached out to thousands of local people. There is a perceptible change in public attitudes around Nagarahole. Two simple facts highlight the project's impact: In earlier years, when forest patrols arrested

poachers, there was public support for the law-breakers. Now there is scarcely any. Second, losing his hated public enemy status, Chinnappa has become a local hero to the majority of the people. His wildlife education 'show' is in constant demand, not only around Nagarahole, but also throughout the district and beyond.

A journalist friend once described Chinnappa as a 'yogi and a commissar'—a label earlier stuck by Arthur Koestler on Mahatma Gandhi. Chinnappa is undoubtedly a tough, efficient, and sometimes cruel, commissar. Yet, at a personal level, his purity, integrity and spartan lifestyle remind us of a true yogi. But I believe there is more to Chinnappa than this simple label. During our friendship of over three decades, I have seen many other facets of his personality: incredible courage in the face of real physical danger, extraordinary knowledge of natural history, deep loyalty to his friends and a schoolboy-like propensity for frequently cracking vulgar jokes, are all a part of his splendid personality.

During most of Chinnappa's lifetime, his towering personality has remained hidden from public view, except to a few close associates. However, the three decades of his accomplishments in Nagarahole are undoubtedly a major milestone in the history of Indian wildlife conservation. There is much that wildlife conservationists can, and should, learn from the life of this remarkable warrior in the jungle.

4
Nagarahole: A World of Predators

IT WAS A WINTER EVENING IN 1973. AFTER a full day's worth of wandering in the forests Chinnappa and I were returning to the camp. The fiery orange sun, about to dip behind the misty-blue Brahmagiri ranges of the Western Ghats, bathed the forest in a golden glow. A roosting peafowl suddenly rocketed off its perch on a leafless tree in front of us. Almost immediately, barely twenty metres ahead of us, a chital doe broke cover, with a single wild dog in pursuit. Neither animal took any notice of us, at the culmination of what apparently had been a long, torrid chase that had left the rest of the dog pack far behind.

The chital had to escape now—before the rest of the pack caught up; the solitary dog had to hold the deer at bay until more help arrived. As we watched, the dog managed to grasp the nose of the deer and pull it down. The wretched animal had already been partially eviscerated, blinded in one eye and had lost an ear during the brutal chase. The deer repeatedly tried to stand up, reeling like a drunk, but collapsed again and again.

Finally, it lay down quietly, its bloodied flanks heaving. The dog let go of its grip: the chase was over. The fierce, and somewhat comical looking, predator now noticed our presence for the first time. It got agitated and moved some distance away.

Tribal people—or even forest staff—would have chased the dog off and appropriated its kill. A man stealing a predator kill has the same effect as a man shooting a prey animal. The pack would then have had to make another kill, doubling its natural impact on prey populations. This dog was expecting us to steal its kill, but was too scared to do anything about it. We moved away quickly to allay its anxiety. Soon the rest of the pack would arrive to consume the hard-earned meal. We had no right to interfere in this natural process.

Of the three large predators in Nagarahole, dholes (or Asiatic wild dogs) are the smallest, weighing only around twenty kilograms. Unlike big cats, dholes not only lack the strength to pull down large prey animals alone but also do not possess the powerful jaw muscles and long canine teeth that can deliver the quick killing bite. Therefore, dholes hunt in packs. They must chase their fleet-footed quarry—usually deer—over long distances, all the time nipping at its flanks, underbelly, ears or tail in an attempt to slow down and weaken it. The prey gradually gets exhausted and is pulled down and killed at the end of a long chase. However, the dense cover of the Indian jungle makes it difficult to watch dholes hunt for any length of time, unlike in African savannahs where the drama of African wild dogs, hyenas and cheetah coursing after their prey can be observed from beginning to end.

I recall one more instance of dholes hunting. It was a weekend afternoon in 1986: not the best time to be in the tourist campus of Nagarahole, jammed with noisy holiday crowds. I sneaked away

towards a forest pool called Hulipatte Kere two kilometres away, to peacefully watch animals that I knew would come to quench their thirst. Scattered throughout Nagarahole forests, there are several such 'keres': storage ponds created by impounding stream flow. The villagers who had built these tanks left centuries ago. The jungle reclaimed their settlements and the keres fell into disrepair. However, the forest department has subsequently repaired some of them to provide water sources for wildlife.

It was 4 p.m. when I commenced my vigil, sitting on the ground leaning against the fat buttressed bole of a *Terminalia bellerica* tree that stood fifty metres away from the pool. I knew that if I managed to stay absolutely still, I would be nearly invisible to the animals that came to drink at the pool. I wore jungle camouflage that broke my outline, hiding me like a leopard's rosettes hide its form in the jungle brush. An open grass swamp, locally known as hadlu— extends northwards from the pool for half a kilometre. Dense moist-forests, fringed by tall bamboos surround the pool and the grassland. The jungle was quiet, except for the lilting calls of hill mynas and the booming of silvery hanuman langur monkeys that kept me awake in the afternoon heat.

About an hour passed. The tranquillity was shattered by the rattle-like alarm calls of a pair of giant squirrels. At the far end of the grassland a herd of five chital broke cover and ran across— with a pack of eight dholes in hot pursuit. Both disappeared into the bamboos. For about three minutes I thought I had lost sight of them for good, and was sorely disappointed at having missed the chance to watch the full sequence of a dhole hunt unfolding before me.

Suddenly, I heard the crackle of *Lantana* bushes and rustle of dry leaves along a trail made by animals—a game path—that extended to my right. As I looked on in amazement, a chital stag rushed down the path right at me, with four dogs chasing it. To race through the jungle brush unimpeded, the stag had raised his chin skywards, holding his cumbersome antlers flat against his flanks so they would not tangle in the brush. His eyes bulged and nostrils flared in terror. I could hear the stag's strained breathing as he sped past me in a flash of tan and white. I could have leaned forward and touched him. The fiery red dogs raced after him, only a few metres behind. Neither prey nor predator had noticed me at all.

Unable to shake off the dogs, the stag tried a desperate gambit. He wheeled and raced across the bund of the pool, and leapt right into the water. Perhaps this strategy of tiring the dogs out would have worked if the water was shallow enough for the deer to stand upright, yet so deep that the short-legged dogs would need to swim to stay afloat. It might then have been easier for the deer to ward off the dog's cruel, snapping jaws by lashing out with its sharp antlers and hooves while it gained its breath. However, this was not to be. The pool was too deep and the stag had to swim to stay afloat. He now decided to swim across and try to escape into the forest on the other side. However, while two dogs jumped into the pool and swam after the stag, the rest of the pack ganged up along the other side of the pool. They paced up and down the bank of the pool trying to cut off the stag's escape route. The desperate stag was forced to swim in circles: the two dogs swam more slowly but kept cutting across the circle to corner the stag. The stag was getting exhausted rapidly. His fate was sealed.

Sensing the imminent kill, the two dogs attacked the stag in the water, tugging at his ears, biting his eyes and pushing him underwater with their feet. One more dog jumped into the water to help them drag the stag ashore for the rest of the pack to attack. It was all over in a few minutes, as the stag emitted a horrific last scream. The dogs started feeding even before he died.

Although all eight dogs must have been hungry and exhausted, there was no serious squabbling of the sort that is evident when several cats feed on a kill. It was a peaceful affair with three or four dogs eating at a time, while the others waited their turn. The dogs almost polished off about forty kilos of edible meat (two-thirds of the carcass) in as many minutes.

Soon their bellies bulged and they lay down panting. Some dogs began to lick and clean up each other's bloodied muzzles. By now the first crows had arrived, and, alerted by their flight patterns, a dozen white-backed vultures had also swooped down. There was not much meat left for these big ungainly birds: only the skull, bigger bones, the rumen sack, entrails and the neatly flayed spotted pelt of the chital remained. The birds flapped their wings and squabbled noisily over these pitiful remains.

One of the dogs decided to take a walk, perhaps to relieve the acute discomfort of its bloated belly. It came very close to the tree under which I sat. Suddenly, recognizing my still form as that of its dreaded enemy, man, the solitary dog retreated quickly, emitting low growls and rejoined the safety of its resting pack. Contrary to popular impression, dholes normally avoid rather than attack any human beings that they may accidentally encounter.

A few minutes later, I saw a herd of gaur emerge from the forest, walking in single file along a game path about ten metres from me. These massive deep brown wild cattle have very poor colour discrimination ability, and simply could not isolate my camouflage-clad form from the brush that surrounded me. They passed within five metres of me, totally unaware of my presence.

The gaur headed straight for the pool, ignoring the dogs. The dogs, however, had different ideas. They dashed around the wild cattle, harassing them playfully. The gaur emitted low growls, but were calm as they drank from the pool deeply and for long. The hungry killers of the stag had turned into playful puppies after their bellies were full. Although dholes do kill gaur calves, it is rare, and possibly happens when calves get isolated from the herd, thus rendered defenceless against predators.

As the sun dipped behind the trees lining the edge of the grassland the dogs loped off into the forest. I got up and walked back to camp, happy at having been a part of their cruel yet beautiful world, even if it was for just a few hours.

Dholes usually hunt during the day, coursing after their prey in open areas. Tigers and leopards, on the other hand, usually stick to denser cover and prefer to ambush their prey between dusk and dawn. These differences ecologically separate the two big cats from the dogs. Observing encounters between these predators is therefore a rare treat for any naturalist.

One morning in 1986, as I drove with Chinnappa along one of the many dirt roads that criss-cross the Nagarahole forests, we saw three dholes resting on the dusty track ahead of us. Although the usual pack size of dholes in Nagarahole is about eight to ten adult dogs, outbreaks of disease periodically cause fluctuations in numbers, sometimes eliminating entire packs. These three animals were remnants of a pack of eight, which had suffered from mange a few months earlier.

The dogs got up, played around with each other for a while and set off at a trot. We drove a few metres behind them at a measured pace, in the hope of seeing them hunt. After about half a kilometre, we heard the harsh alarm barks of langur monkeys emanating from the woods a hundred metres ahead to our left. The dogs stopped in their tracks, fully alert.

The monkeys, who had not seen the dogs, were clearly agitated by something else that was moving in the forest cover below. A few seconds later a large male leopard came out of a game trail, walked onto the road, turned and headed towards the dogs. Having been thwarted by the alert monkeys he had hoped to ambush, the leopard was coming our way, possibly looking for some other prey. The leopard had not noticed the dogs.

I knew that large packs of dogs could chase and even kill a leopard. However, I was curious to know what this pack of only three dogs would do. Clearly they could not kill this sixty-kilogram, fierce big cat on their own.

I was amazed, therefore, when without even a moment of hesitation, the lead dog rushed towards the leopard followed by the other two animals. Surprised out of his wits, the leopard lifted his tail, snarled, and quickly turned and bolted. The cat dashed up a tree, lost his grip and fell down. The dogs swarmed all over him, but the leopard clawed his way out of the melee and bolted through dense forest, with the dogs in hot pursuit. We got out of the car and ran after them. Although we could hear the progress of the chase—via the angry growls of the leopard and the alarm calls of langurs, jungle fowl and squirrels—we simply could not catch up with the speedy antagonists. We returned to the car frustrated, wondering how the chase had ended.

Later the same evening I saw the three dogs a few kilometres away, still hale and hearty. Their suicidal engagement with the big leopard did not seem to have been conclusive. The leopard could have easily confronted three wild dogs. However, the cat's natural instinct of fleeing at first sight of dholes—without stopping to count how many there are—had greater survival value in evolutionary terms. The leopard's vast geographic distribution, stretching from southern Africa to the Russian Far East, the most extensive and varied range among all big cat species, testifies to the animal's evolutionary adaptability as a true survivor.

Records of interactions between tigers and dholes are even fewer. A few old hunters, including Kenneth Anderson, have reported dramatic encounters between packs of thirty or more dogs and tigers. They graphically report battles in which the tiger was eventually killed, despite slaying several dogs in the fight.

I am not sure if these old accounts are totally factual. Usually dholes live in packs of eight to twelve adult animals. After a litter is born, when the pups are old enough to go out hunting, the pack size may temporarily swell to twenty or so animals, before the group splits up. Because of dense cover and the quick movements of the dogs, counting the number of animals in a pack accurately is not always easy. Could these old tales of thirty or more dogs simply be cases of inaccurate counting? Did these old hunters see the full sequence of chases, or had they merely extrapolated from what they saw in bits and pieces like I have described above?

In 1991, I once saw a pack of five dholes unknowingly enter a patch of bamboo in which I knew a tiger was resting: it was an animal that I had radio-collared a year earlier. The tiger's radio signal told me that soon after, the cat had woken up from its slumber. I saw the dogs move away from the bamboo patch a little after they entered it. They must have become aware of the tiger's presence, and decided to avoid a confrontation. The tiger had then gone back to sleep.

Chinnappa told me that he had once seen a tigress with two cubs enter a thicket in which a pack of dholes were feeding on a

chital kill. Following a brief skirmish and some fierce growling, the tigress had appropriated the carcass from the dogs and chased them off. When Chinnappa investigated the kill site later, he found two dead dholes. In another more recent instance, my naturalist friend Harsh Dhanwatey observed two juvenile tiger siblings in Tadoba tiger reserve lounging in a pool of water to ward off the summer heat. When a pack of dholes came out of the edge of the forest, the male tiger had charged without hesitation and driven them off.

An adult tiger can weigh anywhere between 120 and 300 kilograms, or six to fifteen times the size of a dhole. When attacking such a large, dangerous quarry, the dogs will certainly lose several members of the pack. Does such aggressive behaviour have any survival value for dholes? I think not, unless the tiger is seriously injured or sick, and therefore the risk involved in the attack is minimal. My own limited experience suggests that dholes may not instinctively chase tigers as they do leopards. Such caution makes good evolutionary sense.

During the course of my studies I have collected hundreds of scats (droppings) of tigers and leopards to learn more about their feeding habits. The occasional presence of hair from dholes in such scats suggests that these big cats do prey on the dogs, albeit rarely. Perhaps they do so at night, when the dholes rest, and are thus vulnerable to ambush-predation.

Over the years, Nagarahole's forests have provided me with a unique natural laboratory where I learnt how three large predators coexist. These forests have been a wonderful natural laboratory for testing scientific ideas about predators, prey, and their conservation.

I will explore these theoretical questions about predators and prey briefly, in some of the chapters that follow.

Over the last thirty-seven years that I have visited Nagarahole—initially as an amateur naturalist, and after 1986 as a researcher—these jungles have educated as well as entertained me endlessly. More than anything else, it is the cruel beauty of the three large predatory carnivores in Nagarahole—tiger, leopard and dhole—that energizes me. I have no doubt in my mind that these occasional high-voltage encounters with these predators have steeled me to endure the variety of frustrations involved in being a researcher and conservationist simultaneously. Although I am intellectually driven by the urge to explore the dynamics of predation, I must confess that it is the raw physical energy drawn from these predators that has stoked the fire of natural history in my belly.

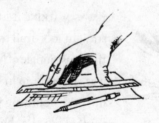

5
The Numbers Game

I WAS WALKING BEHIND PRAVEEN ON A straight foot-trail that cleaved through the dense jungle of Nagarahole. Praveen was a young man volunteering on a mission: counting wild animals. Dusk snuffed out the sharp edges of trees. It was getting late to be walking in these forests crowded with wild elephants. Praveen and I moved noiselessly, trying to sneak up and count the chital, sambar, muntjac, wild pig and gaur on either side of our path, before they could detect us and flee. Our goal was to count all the animals we could see from the trail that we had cut earlier (called a transect line). Most animals we encountered were harmless enough: clusters of dainty chital scattering away with their white under-tails flashing; the majestic sambar with their startled honks of alarm; herds of massive gaur that rolled away like thunder, after a quick snort of surprise.

Elephants, however, were a different matter. Normally shy and retiring animals, elephants could be unpredictable if one blundered into a herd in thick cover. Solitary bulls, or mothers with calves, sometimes charged at intruders. What happened next, as an old jungle hand once told me, was entirely up to the elephant. The fact that every year these elephants in the Nagarahole region trampled to death a few careless farmers and poachers made us all the more wary. However, as long as we detected the elephants before they sensed us, we were reasonably safe.

I was confident that Praveen could be wary and still do a good job of counting. He had heard my repeated instructions to his group of volunteer trainees over the past three days. 'Dress in jungle camouflage which breaks your outline . . . be absolutely alert . . . walk down the trail stealthily, searching the forest ahead carefully . . . when you see a group of animals . . . stop . . . identify the species . . . count them rapidly . . . use your range finder to measure the distance from your position to the centre of the animal group . . . take your compass . . . measure the bearing to the animal group . . . record the data . . . by now the animals may have sensed you and scattered . . . make sure you get the numbers right . . . proceed slowly once again . . . scan the forest for the next group of animals.' I had warned the trainees about the dangers the jungle held for the unwary and the foolhardy: 'This is no picnic. If you blunder into wild elephants, they may panic and attack. Be alert . . . try to see or hear elephants before they detect you . . . no data is worth your life . . .'

When I had begun my field studies of tigers in Nagarahole a few years earlier, I realized that the community of prey animals—deer, pigs and wild cattle—influenced every aspect of the big cat's biology. Therefore, my first goal was to determine how much prey was available as big cat food. However, counting prey animals— seven species of ungulates and two kinds of monkeys—in the dense forests of Nagarahole is a tricky business. It is simply not possible to go out and do a 'census' (count every animal), as one could perhaps with a flock of penguins sitting on an ice floe. The forests are too vast, I could not be everywhere, and dense vegetation limits visibility to a few metres. Most individual animals of the prey species look alike, and one is never sure of not double-counting.

Faced with such seemingly intractable problems, wildlife biologists and biostatisticians the world over have converged on a solution known as population sampling. They now approach the problem of counting animals somewhat like a pollster trying to predict election results without talking to every voter. Since biologists cannot go everywhere, and cannot count every animal even where they can go, they aim at getting a representative sample count, just as the pollster does. With such valid sample count data, biologists can make inferences about the whole population.

In my line transect sample surveys in Nagarahole, animals are counted in representative sample strips of forest to estimate their population density: the estimated number of animals per square kilometre. Even if some animals in the sample strip are not counted because of limited visibility, the distances at which animals are seen can be measured using an instrument known as the range finder. Biologists use these 'distance data' to estimate the *proportion* of animals present in the strip that they actually managed to detect and count. The beauty of the scheme is that the total number of animals can be estimated even when not all animals in the sample area are detected during the survey (that is, the proportion of animals counted falls below 100 per cent). Because of this power, sampling-based approaches to animal counting, like line transect surveys have wide potential utility. Since the 1980s, the development of complex statistical models and availability of speedy computers have greatly empowered biologists doing line transect surveys.

However, even with all this analytic power at his command, a biologist like me who deals with animals that live at low densities over vast forest tracts, must be prepared to do a lot of tough legwork. To get reliable estimates of prey densities in Nagarahole, I had to walk at least 500 kilometres every year. Consequently, during the first year of my study, I spent almost five months just trudging along transect lines to count the tiger's prey animals.

Later, as I expanded my goals to study other aspects of tiger biology, I could spare only two weeks in a year to walk transect lines. However, I realized that I could complete the task in this short period if I had fifteen more trained 'animal counters'. The basic line transect work involved field skills such as rapidly spotting, and accurately identifying and counting animals. It also required the animal counter to correctly use simple instruments like range finders and compasses, and to record the data in set formats. I could not therefore depend on my hardy but essentially illiterate Jenu Kuruba trackers.

Faced with this dilemma, I had an inspiration: Could I possibly train the numerous amateur naturalists who visited Nagarahole and constantly plagued me with requests to take them out into the field? That is how I managed to find Praveen and other members of my first team of volunteer-naturalist recruits.

I selected the first group of trainees after rigorous screening. Long hikes in the forest tested their capacity to survive tough fieldwork. The ability to spot and identify animals quickly, accurately read instruments, record the information carefully, and stoically suffer the bites of ticks that infested the Nagarahole forests: these were

all deemed essential qualities for a recruit. Uncomplaining zeal, steadfastness in dangerous situations and tolerance for spartan camp life were also important criteria for being selected.

In those early years, I faced a high dropout rate among recruits, as youngsters who flocked to Nagarahole seeking Tarzan-like glamour in field biology, wilted quickly in the face of adversities. It was amusing to watch them depart within a day or two, trotting out patently lame excuses: a grandmother suddenly on her deathbed, a business crisis that had erupted with curious suddenness and most often severe diarrhoea that had flared up overnight (usually after an encounter with wild elephants the previous evening). Gradually, as the notoriety of the hardships in my animal survey training camps spread, the proportion of casual thrill-seekers declined and that of serious naturalists increased. The tradition continues to this day, and I have gathered data successfully employing this participatory conservation science in over a dozen tiger study sites across India.

My two-week line transect survey camps offer an exciting experience for the eager volunteers. These volunteer-naturalists come from a variety of backgrounds. Some are college students. Others are young professionals: engineers, computer programmers, businessmen, coffee planters, accountants and teachers. A few are aspiring wildlife biologists, or park rangers deputed by the forest department. Most are avid animal watchers with a passion for the wilderness.

My first task in training them is to demystify the science of counting animals. Because India's foresters, who manage wildlife, lack serious training in wildlife biology, they often promote the absurd idea of a 'census': that one can go out and count every individual tiger or deer in this vast country. I bluntly tell my trainees

that these so called 'censuses' are practically worthless and the resulting 'animal numbers' touted in the media are meaningless. The next three days of training are spent showing the volunteers to do the right things instead: how to sample animal populations using surveys, the field craft of counting animals, recording data and then computing animal density estimates from rigorous field data.

Over the years, a dependable cadre of conservation activists has emerged from among the early volunteers at animal survey training camps. Many now volunteer their time freely to assist research, education and conservation projects I run for the Wildlife Conservation Society in India. For instance, a decade later, Praveen, now an advertising executive, spends more time as an unpaid lobbyist for wildlife than pursuing his profitable profession; Girish is a coffee farmer who tirelessly campaigns for wildlife among his neighbours. Sanath, a retired engineer, is a stern taskmaster on the transect line but also a hot draw at the field camp because of his risqué jokes. Samba, a business graduate, has switched careers to become a wildlife biologist. And Sanjay, an engineer, has done the same to manage conservation projects. All of them are effective at saving wildlife, not only because they care deeply, but also because they think clearly and act decisively when a crisis erupts.

Away from the forests of Nagarahole, I often hear conservation philosophers expound fancy schemes for enthusing 'local people' to save wildlife, schemes which usually involve giving away some resource or the other from a nature reserve as a handout to the people who are supposed to save the reserve. Such schemes, involving piecemeal dismantling of the wilderness itself, to provide economic incentives to local people to conserve wildlife, have very little biological or social sustainability in the long run—as many global assessments now show.

My experience with volunteer-naturalists makes me wary of such clever schemes. Grand plans for 'sustainable use' of nature rarely work unless local people are inspired to care for the wildlife in the first place. Before local people in general can be educated and enthused about saving wildlife, one must build a dedicated cadre of naturalists and conservationists who can advocate the cause of conservation within the local communities. However, mere passion and care for animals cannot turn into effective conservation advocacy. There is perhaps no tool more powerful than practical field biology to inspire naturalists and nurture them to be effective community leaders for wildlife conservation action.

6

Understanding Tigers

PERCHED FIVE METRES UP IN THE fork of a *Randia* tree, I waited, dart gun in hand. Sunlight filtering through the leafy canopy created a harlequin pattern of colour, light, and shade in the brush below. I could hear muted curses as Chinnappa directed my team of trained trackers atop elephants pushing their way through dense bamboo. Somewhere in the space between us, was a tiger sleeping off a meal from a buffalo he had killed the previous night. I was hoping the cat would be disturbed by the elephants, slink away from them, and head towards me. If he did, he would face a three-foot-high barrier of white cloth strung taut across the bushes. Although the 500-pound, lethal predator could effortlessly rip through this flimsy stockade, the stark white cloth against the green jungle would make him wary. He would probably search for a way out around it. If the plan worked, the tiger would eventually emerge through a fifty-foot opening in the quarter-mile-long funnel beneath my

perch, offering me a chance to shoot him with a tranquillizing dart.

Listening for animal alarm calls that would betray the tiger's stealthy passage, I mused about the ingenuity of Nepalese and Bihari shikaris who invented this technique, once employed by royalty to slaughter tigers. Ironically, it is now one of the scientific tools I use to help preserve these big cats. I am looking for answers to some basic questions about the endangered cat: How many can live in a particular forest? What kind of prey do they eat? How long do tigers live? And, above all, how are tigers responding to man-made changes in their environments? To answer these, I need first to be able to follow the cats as they are born, learn hunting skills, disperse, establish territories, find mates, produce offspring, and finally die. To do that, I have had to adopt a new skill: radio-telemetry.

This is why I was perched on a tree in Nagarahole on the morning of 29 January 1990: I was straining every nerve, listening and peering, hoping for a glimpse of that amber shadow.

Minutes before, I had heard the tiger's deep-throated growl of annoyance as the beaters on elephant-back forced him to abandon his kill in a narrow gully. There had been no sign of the tiger since then, not even the cackling of the silver-hackled jungle fowl that usually signals a tiger's approach. Had he turned back and sneaked away between the elephants? Worse, would he bolt down the trail under my tree, ruining any chance of safely darting him? My skills and training, gained under the patient tutelage of Mel Sunquist, a renowned expert on big cats at the University of Florida, were being put to the test.

In the dense cover ahead I suddenly saw a ghostly shadow move. As adrenaline pounded through me, I spotted the tiger: a brief glow of gold as he calmly padded down the trail, massive head swaying from side to side, muscular body a picture of power and grace. My best chance was to get the tiger broadside, through an opening in the cover about three metres away to the right. I slowly swung my dart gun around, hoping his razor-sharp vision would not catch the movement. As his head, shoulder, and flanks appeared in the cross hairs, I squeezed the trigger.

There was a soft plop when the gun shot a red-tailed syringe, which buried itself in the tiger's muscular thigh. He growled, stopped, looked around: 'Damn these stinging bees,' he seemed to mutter. I held my breath. Suspecting nothing, the tiger continued to walk down the trail and out through the gap in the stockade. As he strode out of sight and earshot, I whispered into my walkie-talkie, 'We got him!'

Fifteen minutes later, we found the tiger fully sedated, under a tree. Because he was so handsomely striped and well proportioned, Chinnappa named him Mara, the colloquial Kannada name for the god of love. Soon, radio-transmitter attached to a collar around his neck, Mara joined the three other tigers—Mudka, Sundari, and Dasa—I had radio-collared in Nagarahole earlier that month. All four tigers broadcasted beeps to us that allowed us to keep track of them.

My daily tiger-tracking routine begins at dawn, when I drive up the 900-metre-tall Kuntur Tittu, a hillock at the centre of my study area, to listen to signals from my tigers from a fire watchtower perched on its crest. All through the rest of the day, and sometimes at night, I drive, walk, or ride elephants, criss-crossing the park to keep track of the four tigers as they move long distances silently going about their lives.

Sometimes, when they are out looking for mates, their deep roars reverberate across the landscape. Through the years I have seen tigers in action many times: walking, hunting, mating, and even chasing a leopard up a tree. But most of the day all they do is sleep. Tracking tigers is not all fun and excitement; often it is about as thrilling as land surveying or doing painstaking map and compass work. But entering their secret world has its rewards.

I began my tiger project in the 640-square-kilometre Nagarahole reserve in 1986, supported by the Wildlife Conservation Society and the US Fish and Wildlife Service. I hoped to build on earlier studies by George Schaller in central India during the 1960s and by biologists of the Smithsonian Institution in Nepal in the 1970s and 1980s. These studies had shown that adult females form the core of tiger society, defending somewhat exclusive territories from which other breeding females are excluded, but where sub-adult offspring are tolerated. These tigresses mate with a territorial male who usually has a larger range overlapping those of three females. Young tigers leave their mothers at about two years of age and try to establish their own territories.

When I began my research, little was known about how many prey animals lived in the forests. So, I cut several three-to-four-kilometre-long trails through the Nagarahole forests and repeatedly walked them, counting prey species (see Chapter 5). After walking 500 kilometres and plugging the resulting data into a computer program for analysis, I discovered that the Nagarahole forests are packed with prey at a density of over fifty hoofed animals per square kilometre.

Because the reserve was so rich ecologically (and vigorously protected by Chinnappa and his dedicated staff) Nagarahole's tigers could choose from an astonishing array of food items, ranging from spaniel-sized muntjac deer to gaur that weighs more than a tonne.

To determine what the tigers kill, my trackers and I collected scats—a deceptively neat name for the smelly excreta deposited by the carnivores—and also looked for their kills. After examining hair and bone fragments in 490 tiger scats and looking at 154 tiger kills, I learnt that in Nagarahole, unlike other areas where they prey chiefly on deer, tigers routinely kill adult gaur five times their own weight.

In addition, my radio-tracking revealed that the cats hunt primarily between dusk and dawn, searching in careful broad, zigzag sweeps. They are solitary stalkers, ambushing prey from hiding places. The tremendous initial impact of the cat brings the prey down, and a swift grip on the throat strangles it to death.

I found that prey species were being heavily cropped by tigers, leopards, and wild dogs. Roughly a third of the deer, pig, and gaur in Nagarahole were younger than two years of age. However, their population levels held steady, and tiger numbers were at their highest densities compared to most other tiger populations in India. And there was hardly any livestock evident in the tiger's diet.

I also discovered that Nagarahole tigers had very high death rates resulting from fights for space, kills, and mates. Fewer than half the cubs grow to adulthood. From among these survivors, only about half made it through the fierce competition to reach breeding age.

However, because females breed at the early age of four years and produce three to four offspring every third year, tiger populations could continue to grow if protected from humans. Thus even relatively small tiger reserves in India could maintain thriving tiger populations. Sadly, though, this is not the case in most of the tiger's range. Nagarahole has ten times the density of tigers found in forests only a few miles away.

My studies in Nagarahole suggest that the single most important reason that tigers are scarce over much of Asia is the loss of their prey base. Every day, thousands of villagers enter forests around their homes to shoot, snare, and trap the tiger's favoured food. Except in a few well-protected sanctuaries, such uncontrolled hunting for the pot by local people has driven prey populations down to levels unable to support tigers.

From my data I estimate that a tiger kills once every week or so, taking about fifty animals a year. A mother tiger, however, has to feed her young as well; she needs to take down roughly seventy prey animals a year, most within a short radius of her voracious litter. Thus, to permit an annual 'crop' of fifty prey animals that will support just one tiger, the prey base must number about five hundred prey animals. Therefore, for every fifty deer and pigs killed by villagers in a year, there is prey for one less tiger. In many places now surviving cats are forced to turn to livestock, drawing swift reprisals from people who shoot, snare, and poison the cats, and even burn the forests to kill them.

Only a hundred years ago, tigers ranged from Russia's temperate woodlands to Iran's reed beds, from India's deciduous jungles to Bali's rainforests. Today, they survive precariously in a few patches, having retreated from 95 per cent of their former domain, in the face of relentless human pressures: clearing of land for farming and grazing, woodcutting for fuel and timber, over-hunting of prey, and killing of tigers. Tigers are truly safe only in some well-protected reserves in India and Nepal. Elsewhere, the future of these magnificent felines is uncertain. The fragile ecological web that binds tigers to other living creatures has been seriously ruptured.

In Asian cultures the tiger is a magic symbol, epitomizing power, splendour, and ability. It is also a valuable icon for modern mega-corporations selling profitable products in global markets. Above all, the tiger symbolizes, perhaps more than any other animal, mankind's struggle to protect at least a part of the natural world we share with our fellow creatures. If we act rationally and deploy our resources wisely, I believe there is still time to save the tiger. Will we do so?

Before returning to this and other related conservation issues, I would like to digress a bit, in the next three chapters, into the broader world of predator–prey relationships in nature, so as to set the ecological and evolutionary contexts for the conservation agenda that I advocate in subsequent chapters.

7

Forces that Shape Predation

'SUNDARI' WAS RESTING IN A DENSE PATCH OF bamboo. In the last nine hours of radio-tracking her movements, the changing pulse rate of signals from her radio-collar had told me she had been asleep most of the time, occasionally rolling over or grooming herself before sliding back to sleep. She had reason to be content. She had killed a sambar doe six days before, and fed from the kill for four days, eating ninety kilograms of meat before abandoning the carcass to vultures. For the next two days she had roamed her well-defined home range of fifteen square kilometres in the heart of the Nagarahole forests. I expected that she would now be hungry enough to start hunting again.

At 5.30 p.m., her radio pulses—sounding like the calls of a barbet coming through the portable receiver slung over my shoulder—quickened. The tigress was up and moving! I wheeled my green

jeep around, tracking her invisible movements using a hand-held antenna. She disturbed a jungle fowl that cackled away noisily, and a langur glimpsing her from its perch atop a *Terminalia* tree, let off harsh alarm barks. A herd of chital, hitherto grazing placidly, broke into alarm calls. I saw Sundari cross an open grassy patch, growling in frustration. The chital watched the tigress from about a hundred metres away, ears cocked forward, tails erect, thumping the ground with their feet in a typical display of alarm. Ignoring the hysterical chital, the tigress crossed the dusty track ahead of me and entered the dense forest on the other side. Although I lost sight of her, I was still able to radio-track her movements closely.

I picked up her signals half an hour later, near a salt lick half a kilometre away. Several gaur grazed in the short grass 200 metres away. A two-year-old male gaur ambled along the edge of the clearing, methodically browsing among the bamboo and *Lantana*. The radio signals indicated that the tigress was shadowing his movements hidden in dense cover, but she was still out of attack range. Perhaps the young bull caught her scent, for he suddenly stopped feeding, and cantered away to join his group.

Soon, the tigress emerged at the edge of the cover and resumed stalking. She moved, half crouched, till she found shelter behind an anthill, tensed in a position to launch an attack on the grazing gaur. But there was too much open ground to be covered. Ignoring my vehicle, parked just thirty metres away, she waited immobile for over a quarter of an hour, hoping the gaur would drift towards her as they grazed. But they moved the other way.

Meanwhile, two chital stags, unaware of Sundari's presence, emerged from the cover behind and walked towards her. The tigress sensed their approach and looked back over her shoulder when they were just a few strides away from her. But she could not launch

an attack without turning around, and that meant revealing herself. Making a quick decision, she slunk ahead in a crouch and vanished behind some bushes.

Now Sundari turned around and waited for the chital. Despite her swift move, the chital stags had seen her and dashed off with shrill alarm calls. She got up and looked around with a stoic expression, which seemed to acknowledge that 'life was not easy' for a predator. This was her third successive failure in the last hour and a half. Soon the tigress was on her way again, padding stealthily, ears cocked to detect the faintest noise, her bright amber eyes piercing the enveloping dusk. Her belly was empty and flat, muscle rippled under her tawny striped coat. A perfect predator was on the prowl.

Although the tigress appeared to be designed as the perfect predator, her success rate in catching prey was anything but perfect. Despite the abundance of prey in a home range that packed in more than fifty ungulate prey animals per square kilometre, only about one in every ten hunts she attempted worked. The same forces of natural selection that honed this master predator's hunting tactics have gifted its prey with ways to thwart its designs. It is a finely tuned balance. How did it evolve, and how is it maintained?

We know that plants use minerals from the soil, carbon dioxide from the atmosphere and the sun's energy to make the food that is stored in their tissues. Further up in the food chain are the herbivores, ranging in size from tiny insects to huge whales, which draw on this energy. Predatory animals that kill and feed on other living animals are secondary consumers in this complex web.

A simple fact about predators and prey becomes obvious at this point. If there is not enough prey to go round, predators cannot exist. The fact that complex predator–prey communities have thrived on the earth's changing landscape for millions of years suggests that predators have usually not wiped out their prey base and driven themselves into extinction as a consequence. Is this the result of some grand external design or simply a consequence of natural evolution?

This 'balance' in fact derives from a combination of evolutionary processes and pure chance. Both factors continually act on individual animals in populations of predators as well as their prey. Each individual in a given population differs a bit from the others, both in terms of its genotype (the inherited 'design' of the animal locked up in its genes) and its phenotype (external features such as size, coat colour, behaviour). Because of such differences, the inherent probability of surviving to adulthood and producing offspring varies greatly among different individuals.

Agents of natural selection such as predation, disease, and food supply act on the individual animal. How good a particular phenotype is in coping with these pressures, determines whether the individual survives, reproduces and thereby passes on its 'design' to the next generation. Of course, pure chance too may play a key role in the process, but in the long run, it is the better-adapted individual that is more likely to survive and reproduce.

Although the forces of selection act on the individual animal, they eventually change the underlying genetic make-up of the entire population, because only certain animals survive, reproduce and pass their genes on to the next generation. Thus, from among a population of animals consisting of genetically different individuals, natural selection ultimately favours individuals which possess genes linked to external traits that are better adapted to let them survive and reproduce. Such selective forces continuously sharpen the traits that help predators to be better hunters, survivors,

and reproducers. Simultaneously, similar pressures also enhance the prey's capability to avoid predators, survive, and reproduce. This is an evolutionary arms race between predators and prey: a continuous war without end, a war without victors.

The adaptive traits of both predators and prey are reflected in their physical structure and behaviours. A leopard with a black coat probably has no problem hiding in the dense rainforests of tropical Asia. On the other hand in the dry, open forests the same solid black form would probably be more conspicuous to keen-eyed antelopes or chital. Black leopards are more common in humid forests because they have better chances of surviving and reproducing there than in open forests or savannahs. The leopard's black coat in rainforests is an example of a morphological (relating to physical structure of the animal) adaptation.

Similarly, there are behavioural adaptations. In the open savannahs of Africa, the ecological advantages of hunting in teams, killing larger prey, and defending kills from aggressive competitors, have given rise to group living in lions and hyenas. In the dense forests of Asia or South America, such cooperative hunting may not be feasible for large predators and active defence of kills may be unnecessary. Therefore, the solitary behaviour of the tiger and the jaguar, predators that evolved for life in the dense forests.

Though both morphological and behavioural adaptations are common in nature, not all the traits we see in animals have adaptive values. We must remember that forces of natural selection are active in an evolutionary time-frame. However, predator–prey systems are subjected to variations in climate, vegetation and water availability patterns due to natural, and, increasingly, human-induced factors. Adaptation for one set of conditions may become wholly inadequate if the environment changes rapidly. Unpredictable events can

therefore have a major role in shaping evolution. As palaeontologist Stephen Jay Gould argues, if we could wind back the clock of evolution fully and let it unwind again, it is very likely that radically different kinds of animals—not human beings—could inherit the earth. Gould argues that the utility or otherwise of traits that we now observe in any animal, must be understood in the context of the ecological conditions under which it originally evolved.

The number of animals involved in mutual interactions shapes predator–prey communities. We know that some animals are common and others are rare. Enter any good wildlife reserve in southern India, and it teems with chital. On the other hand, sambar deer are relatively scarce, and tigers even more so. Why? The relative abundance of animals in natural communities is perhaps the single most important factor that influences aspects of predation.

The science of ecology is essentially a game of numbers. Therefore, before examining predator–prey interactions, we need to understand the factors that determine the relative abundance of different species of animals in a natural community. Among these, two loom large: the diet of the animal and its body size. Carnivorous animals that eat rich but relatively scarce food, are usually less numerous than herbivorous animals that subsist on nutritionally poorer but more abundant plant foods. Even among herbivores, those that feed on abundant resources—such as langurs that eat leaves—tend to be more numerous than monkey species like macaques that depend on a richer but scarcer diet of fruits.

Because of their greater food needs, among animal species with comparable diets, larger species will generally be less numerous than smaller ones. Among meat-eaters in a forest, there may be more jungle cats than tigers. Among grass-eating herbivores (grazers), there will be more chital than gaur.

What also affects the abundance of any particular species is its 'social organization', a term that sums up the interrelationships between individuals of different age and sex classes in a population. For example, behaviours such as active defence of exclusive home range areas (territoriality) may introduce variations in abundance patterns we could expect on the basis of diet and body size alone. Such territorial spacing mechanisms may limit densities of species as different as tigers and muntjacs.

Competitive interactions among ecologically similar species may sometimes limit the numbers of the less dominant species. Leopard numbers appear to be limited at several sites, in spite of abundant prey availability, because of competition with tigers.

Considering how important animal numbers are to virtually every aspect of community ecology, wildlife biologists studying predator–prey relations pay a great deal of attention to estimating animal numbers in terms of 'density'. This population density, expressed as number of animals per unit area, is quite different from the 'density' used by a physicist to express the mass of a material per unit volume.

To meet their basic needs of food, shelter, and reproduction, animals have to live in a suitable habitat and work at exploiting the resources available. If the habitat of an animal is its 'address', the niche is its 'profession' through which it exploits resources.

With these basic ideas, we can begin to see how exceedingly complex the ecology of an animal community comprising many predatory and prey species, occupying different niches, living in varied habitats, and occurring at different densities can be. Such predator–prey communities are not merely collections of off-the-shelf animals, but have evolved together over millennia in an intricate and often fragile balance. Even the idea of a 'stable natural

balance' is unreal, since things are constantly changing. In reality, these predator–prey communities can be in one of several possible states of equilibrium.

Before examining predator–prey relations in any detail, a basic question arises. Why are particular predators and prey found in certain regions of the world, but not in others? The historical range of the lion extends from Africa through West Asia into north-western India. The range of the tiger extends from northeast Asia in the opposite direction overlapping with that of the lion at its western extremity. The range of the leopard covers the combined ranges of these two bigger cousins.

As zoologist John Eisenberg explains in his classic on the subject, *The Mammalian Radiations*, the current distribution patterns of animal species arise from the adaptations of their ancestors to niches opened up by past climatic, geological, and vegetation changes. For example, Indian fauna today is a mixture of elements from the past faunas of northern Asia, Africa and Southeast Asia. Its current composition and richness are consequences of factors as diverse as movements of continental plates, volcanic activity, the retreat and advance of glaciers, and the timing of evolutionary radiation of different animal groups.

If we look at communities of large mammals in the Indian subcontinent, we are struck by the variety of predator–prey communities that characterize each natural zone. The mountainous and cold desert fauna of the trans-Himalayan zone has the snow leopard, wolf, and lynx as the top predators, preying on many kinds of wild ungulates like goats, sheep, and yak. In the forested lower-level Himalayan zone, the wolf gives way to the leopard and the tiger, and the prey complement changes to include goral, serow, takin, red deer, musk deer, and sambar. In the flat and arid desert zone of western India, the wolf and the now extinct cheetah are the top predators on a prey base that includes wild ass, chinkara, and black buck. In the dry forests of the semi-arid zone, further eastward, nilgai, four-horned antelope, chital, sambar, and wild boar form the principal prey of a predatory guild consisting of lion, leopard, wolf and tiger, depending on specific localities.

These predators and prey occur in specific habitats because of their morphology, ecology, behaviour, and evolutionary history. Therefore, it is not wise to introduce predators across biogeographic regions into localities where they did not occur previously. The introduction of exotic predators such as cats, dogs, and mongooses have caused mass extinctions of native prey species (and even native predators), particularly in Australia, New Zealand, and in islands of the Pacific and the Caribbean regions.

8

Predation as a Way of Life

GENERALLY, WE THINK OF ANIMALS THAT SUBSIST BY hunting and killing other animals as 'predators'. While the wolf, the leopard, and the shark are clearly considered 'predators', macaques and chimpanzees are not, although they too kill and eat other small animals. Monkeys are generally not considered predators, because most of their food is derived from plants.

The word predator is hard to define scientifically. Zoologists classify cats, dogs, bears, civets, pandas, weasels, raccoons, and hyenas that share a common ancestor, and generally feed on flesh, as carnivores. Not all carnivores, however, are considered predators: only ones that primarily depend on hunting live prey are. The big cats, polar bears, spotted hyenas, wolves, and wild dogs are predators, as are a variety of mustelids and viverrids (weasels, civets, and mongooses). Carnivores like pandas and some bears and civets may pursue non-predatory lifestyles. Animals that prey chiefly on insects (like bats) or eat carrion (like vultures) are not considered predators.

Charismatic predators such as the tiger, lion, leopard, jaguar, wolf, golden eagle, king cobra, great white shark, and killer whales, have all fascinated human cultures for millennia. Our awe of such powerful predators is rooted in our own humble evolutionary origins as minor league scavengers in the African savannahs. The puny human hunter who grandly poses over the body of a dead tiger appears to merely exhibit this deep-rooted sense of inferiority that humans feel in the presence of a mighty predator.

It must be the same awe of predation that has struck modern-day biologists. Scientific curiosity has led to varied questions about predation, many of which are not fully answered yet. How do predators search for, locate, select, capture, and kill prey? What

are the ways in which several predators compete for or share prey resources in their habitats? What is the impact of predation on prey numbers and behaviours? What are the evolutionary explanations for the patterns of predation that we observe in nature today? And, increasingly, why are predators vanishing and how can we save them?

I approach these questions here from the perspective of a wildlife biologist interested in proximate causes of predatory patterns that I observe. This is not to downplay the importance of seeking ultimate evolutionary explanations for these patterns. I think that explaining predator–prey interactions in ecological rather than evolutionary terms is of greater urgency in these critical times. My own interest in larger land mammals undoubtedly colours my account of predators. I have no doubt that predatory interactions involving birds, fish, amphibians, reptiles, and insects are all equally fascinating subjects to biologists who study them.

Because of their charisma and glamour, predators attract more attention than their prey species. Everybody wants to know how many tigers are there in a reserve, but few care about how many deer there are. Even in a major conservation initiative like Project Tiger, while every one fusses on about counting tigers, scant attention is paid to the status of prey animals. Yet prey populations hold the key to the very existence of predators. While prey populations can thrive in the absence of predators, predators cannot survive without their prey.

Some predators typically specialize on a few major prey types, whereas others are generalists that kill a wide range of prey. I found that about 95 per cent of the meat eaten by tiger, leopard, and dhole in Nagarahole came from just five species of prey: gaur, sambar, chital, wild boar, muntjac, and langur monkey. Small prey such as hare, rats, porcupine, and chevrotains were indeed killed, but their biomass contribution (meat consumed) in the diet of large predators is negligible.

All life is about endlessly recycling energy. A predator expends considerable energy in finding and killing each prey. The larger the predator, the greater is the amount of energy spent in this act. This energy expenditure sets limits on the size of prey needed to sustain a predator. It has been estimated that on an average a tiger needs to kill about 3000 kilograms of live prey in a year to survive. Thus, roughly about fifty prey animals weighing about 60 kilograms are needed to sustain a single tiger over a year. Can the tiger survive instead by killing 30,000 rats that weigh 100 grams each? The answer is no: the amount of energy the tiger expends to catch each rat would far exceed the nutritional energy it would get in return. That tiger's fate would be like that of a man who runs a marathon to get a biscuit.

It is not possible for large predators to live off very small prey alone, although they do take such prey if it comes their way. Tigers cannot live off prawns in mangrove swamps devoid of large prey, nor can lions live off grasshoppers in the savannahs, although such small prey may in fact be most abundant.

A predator on the prowl must encounter a prey animal before starting to catch it. The encounter rate between an individual predator and its prey depends significantly on population densities of prey. If there are five chital groups per square kilometre of habitat for every group of sambar, the odds are five to one that the next prey to be encountered by a prowling leopard will be a chital.

The density of the right-sized prey is therefore probably the single most important factor in determining how suitable a habitat is for predators. This is why there is a world of difference between how tigers make a living in Russian forests with two to four large prey per square kilometre and the lifestyles of tigers in prime Indian forests packed with twenty times that prey density.

Finally, although suitable prey may exist at high densities, they may not always be available. In the Serengeti, wildebeests migrate away from the open plains and are simply not available all through the year to the resident lions. Wolves and snow leopards in India that prey on the livestock of nomadic herders may face similar constraints.

Even if the predator finds its prey, often the prey species possess several physical and behavioural defences against predators. Adult elephants, hippos, and rhinos escape predators because they are too big to be tackled successfully by big cats. Some other prey species have developed an arsenal of mechanical and chemical weapons of defence. Porcupines have deadly quills, which they are only too willing to use, as many a blinded leopard or tiger might testify. Pangolins and tortoises possess tough scales or shells. Some weasels squirt a noxious spray of chemicals from their anal glands, to temporarily blind and deter predators. Some reptiles save themselves by losing their tails to predators while they escape, easily growing a new tail later.

Most prey animals have shapes and colours that help them hide or escape from predators. A speckled coat of fawn and white helps animals like the chital or chevrotain to blend with their surroundings in sun-dappled forests. Even the apparently striking coat patterns such as those of a zebra or Malay tapir, in fact, break up the outline of their shape in their specific habitats, and render detection by predators difficult. On the other hand, several insects look like other insect species that are noxious or stingers, to fool potential predators into leaving them alone.

Not all anti-predator defences are morphological. The prey also uses clever behavioural defences to ward off predators.

Prey can gain safety through the habitat they select. The selection of short grass areas by antelopes thwarts the lion by taking away its stalking cover. The choice of extremely steep cliffs by mountain goats to avoid wolves too is an example of such behavioural defences. Chital deer that congregate around tourist camps in several Indian protected areas probably do so to escape from predators.

Although several prey animals sport powerful weapons such as antlers, horns, beaks, and spurs that are highly effective in fights with others of their own kind, these weapons rarely seem to be useful against predators. Chital stags appear to have little use for their sharp antlers against dholes, even when desperately cornered. Similarly, the massive horns of the gaur seem useless against attacking tigers. On the other hand, zebra kicks can disable lions. I once saw a sambar protecting her fawn from dholes just with her flailing front hooves.

Proactive defensive behaviour, where individual members of prey species gang together to counter-attack and chase predators is common to species such as elephants, African buffalo, baboons, and chimpanzees. Such 'mobbing' to deter raptors is quite common among birds. However, as a rule, anti-predator behaviours involve passive defensive mechanisms rather than offence. Prey animals usually hide or flee to escape capture. 'Freezing' in mid-motion to blend with the surroundings is seen in chital fawns, adult muntjac, and several species of ground-dwelling birds. A variation on this freezing theme involves deliberately feigning death, a tactic that works with predators that are biologically programmed to attack moving prey or predators which do not eat carrion. Opossums of course are famous for playing dead, but even large animals like hyenas sometimes resort to this technique.

Escape through fleeing is perhaps the most common anti-predator behaviour. We see it in its purest form in the fleet-footed antelopes and gazelles of the savannahs. These animals reach astonishing speeds exceeding 100 kilometres per hour, and keep going for miles. If the gazelle gets a good head start, even the fastest of predators like cheetahs have little chance of catching it.

Forest animals such as gaur and sambar dash away impulsively at the slightest suspicion of a predators presence. Flocks of duck or pigeons dive rapidly when attacked by falcons. Fleeing gazelles try to shake off chasing predators by twisting, turning, and dodging unpredictably, to gain that split-second advantage which may mean the difference between life and death. Diving into thick cover like a hare, or disappearing down a hole like a rat, or scaling a tree like a monkey, are all behaviours that exemplify flight of one kind or other.

Although group-living behaviour among prey animals is more likely to have evolved as an adaptation for efficiently exploiting food resources, evolutionary theorists argue that reduced predation risk may also have contributed to the evolution of group living. A fundamental evolutionary advantage of group living, as opposed to solitary living, is that the probability of being attacked by a predator that finds the herd is considerably reduced for any one individual.

In addition, each individual in a group benefits from the vigilance of other individuals in detecting predators. Deer alarm calls, foot stamping and tail flashing are all different tactics they use to share information about a predator among group members. Biologists also speculate that in some cases such alarm behaviour may even be directed at a concealed potential predator. Since many ambush predators give up stalking when they are discovered, such pre-emptive signalling may help in flushing out a suspected predator.

Usually a predator attacking grouped prey animals selects its quarry in the early stages of the attack. A large number of animals just mindlessly milling about can confuse an attacking predator in the first critical seconds, making it difficult for it to select a particular individual. Thwarting predation with such behaviour has been reported for wildebeests attacked by lions and for flocks of birds under attack from hawks.

Just as the prey species are equipped with an array of morphological and behavioural defences against predators, the latter too are armed well by nature to counter such defences. Such predatory adaptations can be related either to the morphology of the predator or to its behaviour.

The large canine teeth we see on big cats are a classical example of a morphological adaptation. On the other hand, the group-hunting behaviour of dholes is a behavioural adaptation. It is the fine-tuned combination of these two kinds of evolutionary adaptations that results in the functioning 'design' of the predator.

We must note that a predator genetically inherits behaviours that enable the most effective use of its physical armoury. Predatory behaviour is as much a part of a predator's 'design' as its morphology. A wild dog that attempts to stalk, ambush, and kill by delivering a lethal bite to the throat in the manner of a leopard has little chance of success. Its body simply does not have the powerful, spring-like qualities necessary for stealthy stalking. Nor does it have the powerful jaw muscles, long canines, and grasping claws that would enable it to deliver the killing bite to the prey's throat. In contrast, the wild dog has a lithe body suited for tireless chases and a long narrow muzzle capable of biting its prey on the run, traits that combine to effectively bring the prey animal down from exhaustion and loss of blood.

Perhaps the single most important factor of a predator's basic design is its body size. The largest land predators such as the extinct dinosaur *Tyrannosaurus rex* (of *Jurassic Park* fame), probably weighed over twenty tonnes, and killed other herbivorous dinosaurs four times their own size. During the Miocene (about 25 million years ago), considered to be the golden age of mammalian evolutionary diversity, several elephant-like animals, and giant versions of present-day tapirs, rhinos, hippos, and sloths roamed the earth. A wonderful array of much larger ancestors of present-day cats, dogs, hyenas, and bears preyed upon them.

Keeping pace with the decline in prey size, present-day land predators are much smaller. The biggest of them, the polar bear, weighs about 700 kilograms while the smallest weasels weigh less than one-thousandth as much.

Mammalian predators on land are members of the Order *Carnivora* and belong to the families *Felidae* (cats), *Canidae* (dogs), *Viverridae* (civets and mongooses), *Procyonidae* (raccoons), *Hyaenidae* (hyenas), *Mustelidae* (weasels), and *Ursidae* (bears). Of these, only some big cats can single-handedly kill prey animals much bigger than themselves. Predators such as the tiger, lion, leopard, and puma show extraordinary prowess in killing ungulates that are five to six times their own size. Most predators are built to kill smaller prey.

Apart from possessing the right body size, predators need sensory mechanisms to detect and locate prey. Their senses should be superior to those of their prey, to provide that crucial element of surprise before the attack. Predators may locate prey by detecting its visual image, or vibrations, smell, body warmth or touch. These different sensory capabilities are employed in varied combinations by different predators.

Sighting the prey is important for predators that live on land. Most predators that hunt by sight detect the movement of their prey rather than its still form. Big cats have eyes and neural networks that can gather images even at low light levels, although their ability to discriminate colours is poor. On the other hand, members of the dog family such as wolves and wild dogs have poor vision in low light levels, and hunt primarily during the day. Raptors that hunt by day have acute vision for the visible part of the light spectrum. Note how frequently a kestrel can detect a tiny mouse in the swaying grass far below! On the other hand, owls that hunt at night can see infrared radiations emitted from the warm body of the same mouse.

Sounds are actually vibrations travelling through air or water. Predatory mammals, birds, and some reptiles can pick up these vibrations through their ears to locate prey. Most snakes pick up vibrations from the ground through bones in their bodies. Similarly, the bodies of predatory fish pick up sound vibrations borne through water. The *vibrissae* or whiskers on mammals such as otters and shrews may also be used for sensing vibrations.

Most mammalian predators have large ear flaps that help to funnel sound vibrations into the ear. If you observe a cat hunting, it is easy to see how it moves its ear flaps constantly to locate the source of sounds made by potential prey.

The sense of smell is acute in many land predators, particularly among members of the dog family. Compared to the human nose, a dog's nose has probably forty times more smell-receiving cells! Although cats commonly communicate with each other through scent signals deposited on the ground or in vegetation, they do not appear to use air-borne scents while hunting. Predatory birds

also do not rely on the sense of smell. However, the sense of smell is an important tool for prey detection among predatory fish such as sharks, which operate in murky undersea habitats.

Snakes such as pythons, pit vipers, and rattlesnakes are able to detect temperature changes in their vicinity caused by the presence of warm-blooded prey. The heat receptors around their facial pits or jaws even enable them to locate their prey and strike with deadly accuracy. Some predatory fish detect prey by touching it, or, even tasting it through mobile and taste-sensitive projections on their faces.

However, locating a prey is only the first act in the drama of predation.

After locating a prey the predator has to get close enough to catch the prey. Once again we can see a wide range of predatory strategies. Two strategies however tend to dominate the predator's behaviour of getting within range of a prey.

The first strategy consists of pure ambush. A well-concealed predator waits for the prey to almost bump into it. There are several variants of this strategy of pure ambush. The insect killer, the praying mantis, resembling an innocuous twig or leaf, waits to seize an unwary passing prey. A coiled viper concealed under leaves does the same. Other predators rely on an amazing array of technologies to draw the prey closer. Some spiders weave complex webs, while others build elaborate ground traps. The archer-fish spits out a jet of water as far away as two metres to catch its insect victims, whereas the chameleon darts out a long sticky tongue to ensnare its prey. Sea anemones, jellyfish, and corals demonstrate other variants of the strategy of snaring prey after simply waiting for them to come within range. Usually lower organisms that feed on abundant prey adopt the strategy of pure ambush.

Higher animals that actively hunt for their prey commonly use the second strategy. These hunters are 'stalk-and-ambush' predators like the tiger, leopard, or the lion. Or they are 'coursing predators' like the wolf, wild dog, or the cheetah which run down their prey after fairly long chases. The former have padded feet, perfectly balanced sinuous bodies, heavy builds, the ability to remain motionless for long periods, and the tremendous leaping abilities needed for their deadly ambuscade. The coursers have lighter bodies, long legs with toes and pads built for running, and the great stamina needed to tirelessly chase after their prey.

Strikingly similar to these hunting strategies of land predators are the hunting methods adopted by avian predators. While hawks and hawk-eagles prefer to wait and pounce on passing prey at short range under the forest canopy, falcons prefer a long and rapid chase in the open skies to capture their prey. The former have broad, rounded wings for dodging rapidly through cover, while the latter are equipped with long, pointed wings capable of attaining incredible speeds of over 250 kilometres per hour.

Having caught its prey, the predator has to quickly subdue its victim before it can be consumed safely. As we have already seen, many prey species have formidable anti-predator defences that are capable of inflicting serious damage. Therefore, immobilizing the prey immediately after the attack is vital. Some snakes like the cobra use poison to immobilize prey, whereas others like the python do so by coiling and compression. But most predators use teeth (or beaks) and claws to subdue and kill their prey.

The killing process is comparatively easy if the prey is smaller than the predator. However, if the prey is larger, the predator has to be careful. When bringing down large, hoofed animals, big cats grip the throat, and strive to keep away from the flailing hooves. I

have observed that tigers sometimes hamstring adult gaur to disable them before killing them.

Mammalian predators have sharp canine teeth specifically designed for puncturing the windpipe, severing blood vessels or ripping open the belly of the prey. Most spectacular examples of such specialized teeth were seen in the extinct sabre-toothed cats that hunted large, thick-skinned elephants, rhinos, and sloths. Most predators have sharp, hooked claws that are used to grip and manipulate prey while delivering lethal bites.

The feeding structures and the digestive systems of predators vary considerably. The cheek teeth of cats and dogs are designed for shearing off chunks of meat before swallowing them. Carrion-eating hyenas sport the biggest cheek teeth, specially adapted to cracking large bones. On the other hand, predators that only eat small, soft prey items, such as insects, usually lack strong shearing teeth.

A predator's diet of meat is nutritionally richer than the diet of herbivores. Therefore, compared to any herbivore that has to feed continuously on large quantities of forage, a predator of comparable body size can go without food for several days. The stomach and the gut of a predator are relatively compact, allowing for a lighter, 'sporty' body that suits its predatory life. However, finding and catching prey involves much more effort than finding plants to feed on. Furthermore, successful prey capture is a chancy event. Predators have therefore evolved digestive systems that can adapt to a feast-or-famine regime. A tiger may spend eighteen hours of the day sleeping, and kill only once in a week. However, it is capable of eating one-fifth of its own body weight in a single meal.

From what we have seen earlier, it is clear that predator–prey interactions are complex. They are also influenced by the ecological

interplay between prey populations and their food resources, as well as by interactions among competing predators. Predator–prey relations remain poorly understood in most ecosystems, even to this day. Despite several years of scientific research, the role of predation in regulating prey populations still remains unclear. However, the available data suggest that many popular notions about predators, prey, and 'the balance of nature' may be too simplistic.

One of the most important aspects of predation is prey selection. The prey population consists of several different species of prey. Within each species there are variations between individual animals because of differences in age, sex, and reproductive condition. A predator is said to be 'selecting' prey if it hunts animals of a particular species (or age-sex category) disproportionately in relation to the numbers of such prey types.

Do predators select only 'unfit individuals' among prey, thus maintaining the health of the prey populations as often believed? If so, only old prey animals past their reproductive prime, or diseased and injured individuals should get hunted. There is some evidence that when adverse climate or diseases disable large numbers of prey, predators preferentially kill unfit individuals. I observed a heavy incidence of tiger predation on gaur that were affected by foot-and-mouth disease in Nagarahole. However, most field studies of large predators show that while predators do take unfit individuals, they appear to prey heavily upon young animals, gravid females and even prime males.

Young prey is less experienced in escaping from predators. Gravid females are handicapped by the weight of their foetuses. Adult male ungulates tend to be solitary, a behaviour which increases each individual's chance of meeting a predator on the prowl, as well as

depriving it of the benefit from the group's vigilance. Male deer in hard-antler are thought to be less attentive during rut and may even be more conspicuous targets for attack. The point is simply this: predators take prey that they can easily catch, rather than 'weeding out the unfit' as is sometimes popularly believed.

A factor that influences the prey selection process strongly is the size of prey. As we saw earlier, it is more 'profitable' for predators to select the largest prey they can safely catch. Biologists have reported evidence of such energy-maximizing foraging tactics among African lions. In Nagarahole National Park, I observed that the tiger selected the less numerous but larger-sized gaur and sambar in preference to the much more abundant chital. However, where large prey is scarce, tigers select chital—as observed by George Schaller in Kanha National Park of India and by Mel Sunquist in Chitwan Park, Nepal. In Thailand, however, due to the elimination of large-sized prey by human hunters, tigers may subsist by killing even smaller prey like muntjacs.

In the long run, predators have to 'crop' available prey populations in a sustainable manner. This 'sustainable harvest' does not result from any planning on the part of predators. Although predators generally do not kill more than what they need, there are occasional reports of surplus predation. Such aberrant behaviour occurs when the killer instincts of predators are triggered off by the helplessness of the prey that is unable to escape for some reason. Ecologist Hans Kruuk reported such an incident in which a spotted hyena pack wastefully killed 110 Thomson's gazelles trapped in a rainstorm. Tigers or leopards that get into cattle pens sometimes rampage similarly.

If predators increase to numbers beyond what the prey base can

sustain, they can sometimes drive prey populations down drastically. Though uncommon, such catastrophic impacts have occasionally been reported, particularly from isolated islands or parks, where temporary surpluses in predator populations have occurred because predators could not disperse out of the area. Monitoring predator and prey populations closely in our nature reserves is vital for this reason.

What proportion of standing prey numbers is killed each year by predators? My studies in several Indian tiger reserves suggest that predators may crop about 15 per cent of the standing prey numbers annually. Ecologist Louise Emmons, working in Peruvian rainforests, found that a medium-sized cat like the ocelot annually crops as much as 40 per cent of its fast-reproducing rodent prey base. The social behaviour of predators, such as defence of territories to exclude other breeding animals, and the long-distance dispersal of newly independent young, usually keep predator densities within limits set by prey availability. If prey becomes scarce due to any reason, predator survival and reproduction rates decline, ultimately reducing predator numbers.

Studies in North America and the African savannahs suggest that mortality of prey species because of factors like adverse climate or disease may be important in controlling the numbers of prey species. On the other hand, in the more even climate of tropical forest habitats predation may have a considerably greater regulatory role. Generally, the evidence from field studies suggests that populations of prey species that occur at relatively low densities are more likely to be regulated by predators, whereas more abundant prey species, such as wildebeest or chital, may be regulated by food supply or diseases.

There is compelling scientific evidence to show that prey densities largely determine how many predators can be supported in a given habitat. Predators have evolved as perfect killing machines. These killing machines are fuelled directly by the prey animals they consume. As such the role of prey in the predator's ecology cannot be overemphasized.

9
Predators and Humans

THE TYPICAL MAMMALIAN PREDATOR'S DIET OF MEAT imposes severe ecological constraints on it. Even an old, partially disabled herbivore may be able to prolong its life by consuming whatever forage it can access. It may thus be able to ward off death by starvation for months or even years. The large numbers of India's much-revered domestic cattle are living examples of this process! On the contrary, a disabled predator meets with an immediate, brutal death from starvation. A 240 kilogram male tiger, I radio-collared in Nagarahole, starved to death within three months of being injured in a fight with another tiger.

Because of the need to hunt effectively, a pregnant predator cannot afford to carry around a large foetus in her womb. For example, although a 50 kilogram chital doe has a gestation period of eight months, a tigress that is three times bigger gives birth in just 105 days. Consequently, tiger cubs are small and helpless at

birth. They cannot escape from danger on their own for quite a while, unlike newborn deer that can flee from danger within hours of being born. These young deer can independently forage on vegetation within weeks, as opposed to tiger cubs that depend entirely on their mother for fifteen months or more.

This dependence of her helpless young has major consequences for the tigress's predatory lifestyle. First, she can raise cubs only in prey-rich areas where she is reasonably sure of catching sufficient prey to meet their heavy demands. A tigress with three large cubs has to kill twice as much as she would to feed just herself. Second, her hunting activity is restricted to areas within easy reach of her litter.

Therefore, although an individual predator may just about manage to survive in areas of low prey density, availability of prey-rich habitat is the key to successful reproduction, and, consequently, to the long-time survival of viable predator populations. Such ecological constraints on predators have important implications for their conservation in an overcrowded world.

Predators fascinate most people. A fair number of us even understand that predators are at the apex of biotic communities, and not mere cultural symbols. They provide us with an excellent gauge for the overall health of the ecosystem that we inhabit. Predator conservation is one of the most practical ways of preserving entire biological communities. Predators are like a protective umbrella under which all biodiversity thrives.

Although most people readily appreciate these basic principles, relatively few understand the practicalities of predator conservation in the real world. Thus, the naïve idea that predators and people can harmoniously coexist inside conservation areas without any conflict with humans has gained ground. But contradictions between the ecology of humans and predators, both mammals with somewhat similar diets, dictate a different reality.

Although predators like lions, tigers, and jaguars have been glamorized in religion and art by human cultures worldwide, there is no doubt that man and predators have been serious competitors throughout history. The reasons are not far to seek. In the distant past, human ancestors like the *Australopithecus* roamed the African savannahs in social bands much like baboons and hyenas do to this day. They must have lived in constant fear of the large predators that shared their habitat. It is unlikely that our primitive ancestors exerted any serious hunting pressure on predators. But by being large, omnivorous mammals, humans also hunted the same prey animals. It is likely that they also stole predator kills, and were sometimes preyed upon by the predators. Because of this ecological competition for the same prey base, humans and predators had an adversarial relationship. Comparisons of prey killed by predators and by primitive hunters show both of them competed for the same prey base. This is evident even today, where such hunting societies survive in Africa.

Following human cultural and technological advances, such as the inventions of fire, tools and later agriculture, the evolutionary dice got loaded in favour of humans. Through large-scale habitat modification, humans were able to exclude their most serious predatory competitors from their settlements.

With the advent of pastoral human cultures, the conflict between predators and humans intensified. However, their new weapons helped humans to hold predators at bay. Finally, with the advent of firearms and other products of the industrial revolution, humans established complete dominance over predators. All over the world, governments offered bounties for killing predators. Predators were finally, and irrevocably, in retreat.

There is a commonly held notion that predators are dangerous animals that habitually attack people. Actually, over the last several centuries, predators have come to greatly fear humans. Their behaviour has long been shaped by evolution to shun humans and flee from them. After being persecuted and harassed over centuries, a tiger today simply does not view a man as it does a cow: its instinctive behaviour of hiding and fleeing from humans is just too strong. It is for this simple reason that thousands of people are able live in daily proximity to large predators such as the big cats, wolves, wild dogs, hyenas, and bears, all over the world. It is by avoiding humans, and not by attacking them, that these predators have managed to survive to this day.

The occasional man-eating tiger or leopard is an aberration. Such man-killing usually results from a freak accidental contact of an injured, starving, inexperienced or hungry predator with a human being in a vulnerable position. However, having once discovered human vulnerability, the quick-learning predator may lose its instinctive fear of humans and start viewing people as simply another abundant prey species. Sometimes, such predatory behaviour may be passed down from mother to offspring, leading to endemic man-eating problems as in the case of the tigers of the Sundarban. Whatever its cause, preying on humans is not at all typical of any predator species.

Over the past centuries, expanding agriculture has changed the face of the land. Extensive jungles, savannah and swamps have been converted to human habitation. In the process, humans have destroyed predators' habitats, eliminated their prey base, and come into increasing conflict with them. As a result, in countries like India, barely three per cent of the land area is now designated specifically as wildlife refuges. Out this tiny fraction of land, probably only half comprises areas suitable for large predators. Even within these last refuges, rapidly increasing human impact is jeopardizing the very survival of natural predator–prey systems. The pressures that people living in and around our protected areas exercise on predator populations are many and varied.

Although spectacular hauls of illegally hunted tiger skins and bones that make headlines in the press cannot be ignored, the reality is that the persistent and widespread poaching of prey species poses a far more serious threat to predator survival. Poachers of prey animals come in all hues: the local villager misusing his crop-protection gun, the adivasi with his snares, traps, nets and other traditional techniques; the small-town poacher who arrives in a jeep, shotgun in hand; and sometimes even affluent urban delinquents, like film stars. Most poachers usually sell what they kill, either in local or distant illegal markets that are virtually bottomless pits. Consequently, poaching depresses prey densities. Eventually prey densities drop to levels at which predators cannot find enough prey to reproduce successfully.

The prey base on which predators depend also gets destroyed through competition with rapidly increasing livestock populations. Cows, buffaloes, goats, and sheep are increasingly taking over the foraging ranges of the rhino, wild buffalo, gaur, deer, antelopes, wild goats, and wild sheep. Unlike wild ungulate communities, which have evolved adaptations to subsist on plant resources in a sustainable manner, domestic animals overload, modify, and damage natural vegetation rapidly. They can extirpate their wild competitors through forage depletion and contagious diseases.

In addition, wild prey species have to contend with damage and disturbance from activities such as the exploitation of fuel wood, timber and non-timber forest produce. Frequent forest fires, lit by people to promote cattle grazing or to facilitate non-timber forest

product collection, degrade the habitat of the prey. As densities of wild prey decline, predators are driven to local extinction.

Predators usually show some form of territorial behaviour in which breeding individuals (or social groups) actively defend home ranges from others of their own species. Under such conditions, inbreeding among close relatives is often mitigated through dispersal movements of sub-adult animals into distant new populations. However, on account of habitat fragmentation and isolation caused by humans, such movement between predator populations is being drastically restricted. Coupled with the fact that predator populations necessarily occur at very low densities (100 square kilometres of prime habitat may hold only 10 tigers as opposed to 5000 chital), such habitat fragmentation can result in reduced genetic diversity. These potential genetic threats cannot be ignored. Some scientists believe that, in the long run, such bottlenecks in gene flow pose serious threats of extinction by reducing fertility, increasing cub mortality and by diminishing the adaptability of predator populations to future environmental changes.

If we reflect soberly on the above factors, we begin to see how complex the issue of predator conservation really is. There is no way it can be achieved without some interference with prevailing human activities. Essentially, predator conservation requires that human needs of land for agriculture and pasture, as well as requirements of timber, fuel wood, dairy and meat products must be generated from landscapes outside predator conservation areas. Can we achieve these goals?

I believe, we still can, if we are clear about a few fundamental issues at stake.

First of all, we have to recognize that at least in protected habitats set aside for predator conservation, increasing numbers of people and livestock cannot coexist with predators. It is more logical to adequately rehabilitate such people outside protected areas. Only then can biotic pressures be controlled, and perpetually escalating conflict avoided. If society is unable to establish predator conservation areas free of incompatible human land uses, then it must accept the likelihood of early extinction of large predators, possibly followed by that of many other creatures later.

Second, even if the fuel, timber, and fodder needs of local people are met through imaginative schemes of land restoration outside the protected areas, a social minority consisting of criminals will continue to illegally hunt or ravage protected reserves. Such elements will always have to be stopped with the only language they understand—effective use of force.

Third, wherever predator conservation efforts bear fruit and their breeding populations get established, human–predator conflict will follow on the edges of such protected areas. In such cases, locally surplus predators have to be eliminated through an effective programme, to neutralize local peoples' animosity towards problem predators. In such contexts, the conservation focus should be on saving the predator species involved, not on being 'kind' to every individual predator involved in every conflict situation.

Fourth, having interfered with natural predator–prey systems for thousands of years by modifying their landscapes and habitats, we now cannot afford a totally 'leave nature alone' philosophy of predator preservation. There is an urgent need to accurately monitor how predator and prey populations are responding to natural and human-induced habitat changes, and to tailor wildlife management practices to achieve conservation goals. Such rational wildlife management can only be based on a solid foundation of ecological information collected using acceptable scientific methods.

The neglect of wildlife sciences entrenched in our present wildlife management policies should give way to a more enlightened approach.

Since predators or their prey cannot lobby, agitate or vote to protect their homes, ensuring their survival is going to be tough. Parroting sentimental clichés about 'people living in traditional harmony with tigers' is not going to help us solve any of the thorny, real problems. At this critical juncture, effective predator conservation requires strong political commitment on the part of the government. Such commitment has to be backed by conservationists who should try to educate the public with hard facts—rather than sentimental fiction—about predators, prey, and the balance of nature.

The challenge of what we can, and cannot, do in our efforts to save India's national animal, the tiger, provides an excellent example of the dilemmas of predator conservation that we have explored in this essay. The next essay probes these issues by asking a specific question: Can we indeed save the Indian tiger?

10

Can We Save the Tiger?

ALTHOUGH I HAVE TRIED HARD OVER the years to be the dispassionate scientist when studying tigers, every time I actually see a wild tiger, I feel a surge of distinctly passionate excitement. The tiger is a truly magical animal to behold: it instantly makes me feel in my bones the raw wildness of nature from which I too was born. With its fearsome power and graceful form overlaid with its striped, tawny-and-white pelage, it is hardly surprising that the tiger has deeply influenced the human psyche across a vast region stretching from the reed-beds of Iran to the rainforests of Indonesia, from the snowbound Russian Taiga to the sweltering deciduous forests of India. As a result, the tiger is deeply embedded in the religions, myths, and iconographies of this ancient tract of land.

Ironically, despite this cultural fascination with the animal, throughout history, tigers and humans have been serious adversaries. The tiger began as a biologically superior contender in this contest,

but as agriculture, technology, and commerce enabled humans to hunt tigers and transform their environment, the animal steadily lost ground to man in the grim battle for survival. Today tiger landscapes have shrunk to less than 5 per cent of their vast former range that spanned much of Asia. Even here tigers are battling for survival, with effective protected areas covering less than 1 per cent of their former range. If we do not act decisively in the next few years, wild tigers will lose ground even further and may eventually be driven to extinction for all practical purposes.

Clearly, before it is too late, we need to examine not only why, but also how we should go about trying to save the big cat.

Reversing the steep decline and recovering wild tiger populations will not be easy. The conflict between humans and tigers is real and is driven by the basic ecology of both species. Human beings covet the tiger's habitat as much-needed land for expanding agriculture; they view the tiger's forests as timber and other forest products; and the tiger's prey as food for themselves. On the other hand, wherever the two live in proximity, driven by their predatory biology, tigers readily kill domestic stock, and occasionally even humans. We cannot wish away the fact that saving tigers will require human society to sacrifice some of its immediate interests. Why should humans do so? I believe there are several good reasons, and try to explore them as dispassionately as I can.

Arresting the loss of 'biodiversity' (a short-cut term for all plant and animal life on earth) is now scientifically acknowledged to hold the key to human welfare in the future. Across the world, nations and political regimes—otherwise holding opposing views on almost everything else—agree that arresting the loss of biodiversity is their top priority for this century. This global social and political consensus has crystallized during the past two decades, based not

on sentimentality but on accumulating scientific evidence and economic arguments.

There is also now a scientific consensus that only a small fraction of the richness of living forms can be saved *ex-situ*, in zoos, arboretums, and laboratories (a means of avoiding the messy conflict between human interests and wild land preservation). Much of the diversity of life on earth needs to be protected *in situ*, in special protected areas earmarked for nature conservation.

There are too many species, interconnected in too many ways that we don't even know about. The ways in which they interact among themselves may contribute to the stability and functioning of the entire biosphere. Because of this precautionary principle, we should try to save tigers, their prey, and the forests that harbour them: just to ensure that we don't lose potentially useful life forms that may provide us the food, fuel, fibres, and medicines of the future. Tiger landscapes are wonderful, unexplored libraries of nature from which we can learn and even profit: degrading them for some immediate but minor gain is exactly like the act of burning an ancient library filled with irreplaceable manuscripts.

Sometimes conservationists plead that the watershed services provided by tiger habitats are also a strong reason for saving tigers. Although a purely utilitarian hydrologist may counter this argument by saying man-made plantations too can protect watersheds, the central point is that natural, intact, plant and animal communities provide watershed as well as biodiversity services.

Some conservationists also point out that by saving tigers (and other wildlife) we can sustain a large eco-tourism industry that can potentially provide far more jobs and other benefits to local people perennially, compared to the unsustainable short-term gains from encroaching on tiger lands. Although cynics may say we see little evidence for this beneficial face of wildlife tourism in India, the experience from many African countries indeed shows that such tourism (including 'safari hunting') can sometimes be a far more productive way of using the land than marginal farming. As agriculture becomes more commercialized in the future, and areas devoted to wild nature dwindle, this is even more likely to be true.

However, going beyond such human-centred, utilitarian arguments, I believe there are ethical compulsions too. Tigers and their habitats are products of millions of years of natural evolution that occurred before *Homo sapiens* evolved a couple of hundred thousand years ago. Within the last few thousand years, human activities so dominated the earth that many products of earlier natural evolution have been exterminated once and for all. Do a few generations of late arrivals like us have any moral right to do this?

I would argue therefore that we must make serious attempts to save tigers and other fragile forms of biodiversity for both practical and ethical reasons. Before we ask ourselves how tigers can be saved, we need to understand their ecology.

Tigers evolved about two million years ago in what is southern China today. All the living tigers belong to one species, *Panthera tigris*. Scientists disagree on how many subspecies (races) of tigers still survive. Some argue that although there is a great deal of physical variation across their range, all tigers on mainland Asia belong to one subspecies; and those on the island of Sumatra to a second one. Others contend, based on recent molecular evidence, that there are a total of nine subspecies. Whoever is right, the tragic fact is that wild forms of tigers that once roamed Southern China, the Caspian region, Java and Bali are all extinct today.

The tigers in India and the Russian Far East are the biggest, with adult males growing to a length of three metres and weighing up to 275 kilograms. Despite great regional differences, tigers everywhere are basically adapted to hunt large, hoofed prey animals weighing between 20 and 1000 kilograms: many deer species, wild pig, tapir, water buffalo, banteng, gaur, and occasionally even rhino or elephant calves. To survive through a year of its life, a tiger has to kill about forty to sixty such prey animals. Therefore, to maintain a steady supply of food to support a living tiger, a prey base of five hundred or more animals is required. In richer tiger habitats of the Indian subcontinent, this prey requirement translates into 10 or 20 square kilometre areas to support a single tigress raising her cubs. In the poorer habitats of the temperate forests in Russia or the tropical rainforests or mangroves of tropical Asia, where prey are less abundant, the area required to support the same tigress may be ten to twenty times larger.

However, productive tiger land is much sought after by humans for farming and pasture, resulting in conflict. The tiger's original range has as a consequence now shrunk by over 95 per cent. More recently, economic development and industrialization to meet ever-increasing human demands have further aggravated these pressures. Biologists have identified several proximate causes for the tigers' dramatic decline: loss of habitat due to conflicting land uses, over-hunting of the tiger's prey species by people, and killing of tigers to protect livestock or to meet the commercial demand for tiger body parts.

However, the fascination of human cultures with tigers—Asian royalty as well as modern corporations have the tiger as their mascot—has inspired a global rearguard battle during the past quarter century to save tigers from extinction. International non-profit conservation agencies have been at the forefront of gathering data on the tiger's plight and trying to attract world attention.

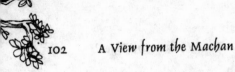

Dedicated individual conservationists as well as institutions located in some of the thirteen tiger range countries in Asia have also fought a tenacious battle to stop the decline of the tiger. Many Asian governments, particularly those of India, Nepal, and Russia, have made determined efforts to set aside protected areas for tigers and enforce laws to keep these areas relatively inviolate from human pressures. Governmental, private and corporate donors from the developed world have also chipped in, investing substantial resources to save wild tigers for the benefit of future generations.

Although tigers breed prolifically in captivity and thrive in many zoos, this fact in itself is not very useful for saving wild tigers. To survive in the long run, wild tigers need large stretches of prime habitat packed with ungulate prey, and relatively free of human interference. Such habitat patches are becoming increasingly scarce in the tiger's range. Therefore, protecting habitats, rather than re-introducing captive tigers, is the core conservation issue.

To ensure the survival of wild tigers in the face of different types of risks, it is necessary to have several large wild populations, each with at least twenty or thirty breeding females. Furthermore, it is essential to have landscape connectivity between such populations to ensure adequate flow of genes among them. Managing tigers in large landscapes that are heavily impacted by human use is not an easy task. So tiger populations of the future have to be managed using many tools from the conservationist's kit. Inspiring cultural tolerance and compassion for the species has to be combined with appropriate economic and social management strategies. Yet, even if we deploy all these social tools of conservation, they can be effective only if they rest on a foundation of solid biological knowledge about wild tigers. The lack of reliable knowledge about tiger biology and conservation requirements has been a major hurdle. How we can find out if we are succeeding or

failing in our efforts to save the magnificent cat from extinction is explored in Chapter 11.

After several years of research in a dozen tiger reserves, a technique known as camera-trap sampling has enabled me to reliably estimate that prime tiger habitats in India can support fifteen to twenty tigers per 100 square kilometres. However, these high tiger densities can drop by 90 per cent or more, if prey species are hunted down to low levels.

These tiger density estimates have several conservation implications: they suggest that, given adequate protection, even the relatively small area available now for wild tigers can support viable tiger populations well into this century and beyond. It is estimated that there are over 400,000 square kilometres of forests potentially suitable for tigers in the Indian subcontinent alone. In an ideal world, if all these potential tiger habitats were to be as well protected as some of our best tiger reserves currently are, the Indian subcontinent alone could support 50,000 wild tigers. Extending the scenario to all of Asia, we can even visualize a world with a 100,000 tigers!

The question that remains is whether we humans will use our great intelligence, massive resources and uncertain wisdom, to act in time to protect tigers in these last remnants of the natural world that gave birth to us. As George Schaller cautioned us eloquently: 'Future generations will be truly saddened, if this century has so little wisdom, compassion, such lack of generosity of spirit, that it eliminates one of the most dramatic animals that has ever lived on this planet.'

Because the tiger has inspired our own civilization and culture so deeply over millennia, I remain optimistic that the world will heed Schaller's impassioned plea before it is too late.

II
The Many Ways to Count a Cat

WHEN I FINISHED SUMMARIZING MY research work for his benefit, the greying senior official from the environment ministry looked at me with wizened, sad eyes. 'I have no doubt, Dr Karanth, that your work is challenging and scientifically important. However, what I cannot comprehend is, how such research can help in saving our poor wild animals? After all, what they need is protection—to be left alone.' Although he spoke in a gentle, civilized tone, I was reminded of a querulous reprimand I had received from a Karnataka politician a few years earlier: 'Why should Karanth study tigers? After all, can his research turn tigers into foxes or oxen?'

Because the bureaucrat had administered several public enterprises in his career, I thought it best to answer him with an analogy drawn from his own domain. I explained that conserving wildlife was in many ways similar to running a large and complex business enterprise. It involves management of nature as well as dealing with people who have different interests, such as forest

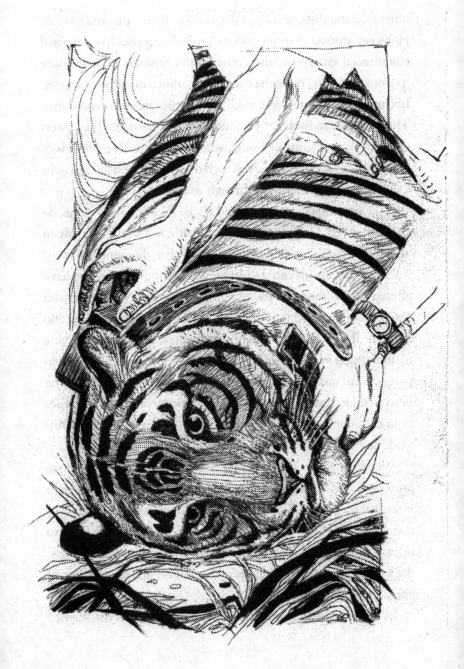

officials, naturalists, adivasis, villagers, social activists, and tourists. However, instead of measuring its 'profits' in rupees like a normal commercial enterprise, the conservation business must measure its gains (or losses) using the currency of animal numbers or species. In this complex enterprise, wildlife scientists are the accountants. They are the auditors for the conservation business: they assess whether it is profiting or losing, whether it is moving towards or away from its original goals. Although the bureaucrat nodded wisely, I am not sure whether I got through to him.

Take for instance the hallowed cliché 'Leave nature alone, do not manage it.' Unfortunately, it is a little too late in the day to accept this fine sentiment at face value. For thousands of years, since we humans invented fire, agriculture, and industry, we have altered the chemistry of the earth, fragmented its landscapes and severely depleted wildlife species, populations, communities, and habitats. If we simply leave nature well alone now, without trying to understand what is happening to it as a consequence of our own past actions, much of the diversity of life may be lost forever. The need to understand—and if necessary, to intervene wisely—arises from this simple truth. The role of wildlife science is to infuse this wisdom into managerial interventions.

Wisely or not, wildlife managers usually intervene for three primary reasons. First, to stop damage from wild animals to human interests; for example, killing or capturing man-eating tigers or marauding elephants. Second, some wild species are harvested to meet human needs, as with oceanic fisheries. Third, increasingly, the wildlife manager's goal has been to preserve and recover animal populations that are in decline.

In all these aspects of wildlife management, it is the science

of wildlife biology that provides the basic underpinning of the knowledge and predictive capacity that makes informed choices from among different management options possible. In the past, management interventions made without adequate scientific input have led to the collapse of major oceanic fisheries, increased elephant damage to crops in southern India, and caused the rapid decline of many endangered species the world over.

Wildlife Biology (now popularly known as Conservation Biology) is a relatively young science. It is an applied discipline, similar to engineering or medicine. Just as engineers draw upon basic sciences like physics, chemistry, and mathematics to solve real-world problems through technology, wildlife biologists try to solve conservation problems drawing on basic sciences like animal behaviour and ecology. In this quest they are now going even farther afield, into the realms of statistics, information theory, computer sciences, geography, anthropology, and social sciences.

However, it is of critical importance to recognize that old-style natural history and field craft—the domain of traditional hunters, collectors, and naturalists—still forms the backbone of modern wildlife biology. Modern wildlife biologists who lack natural history skills are likely to misidentify species, make faulty observations or erroneous measurements, and arrive at predictably wrong conclusions, however sophisticated their analytic skills may be.

For example, a group of scientists once compared tiger paw-print tracings from two different reserves using complex statistical analyses to come up with a suggestion that, on an average, the tigers in one of the reserves were bigger. The biological reason why tigers should be of different sizes just a few hundred miles apart is difficult to comprehend. Yet, someone with greater knowledge of field-tracking tigers might have come up with a better explanation for the measurements: the soil in one of the reserves could have been softer, resulting in, on an average, larger track patterns.

In the worst case, lack of field skills may terminate the research itself, if the hapless biologist blunders into an irate elephant or an angry rhino. Detecting jungle sounds, recognizing and reading animal cues, handling rotting carcasses or animal droppings, and trudging through rough terrain, are all integral to good wildlife biology and simply cannot be learnt in classrooms. Therefore, unlike in many other sciences, stand-alone intellectual brilliance is usually not enough to make anyone a truly insightful wildlife scientist.

On the other hand, good old natural history, on its own, is not wildlife science either. Take for instance the endless hours of observations on tigers collected and published over the centuries by hundreds of hunters and amateur naturalists, assisted by the finest shikaris. After ploughing through all this tiger lore, the reader still remains pretty ignorant about the animal. How much space do tigers use? How do they share space and other resources? How often do they kill and how much prey do they need? How do they budget their time? How long do they live? How is tiger society structured? These questions remained unanswered—all our natural history literature notwithstanding.

On the contrary, within a decade of starting the quest, wildlife biologists like George Schaller, John Seidensticker, Mel Sunquist, and David Smith had the basic answers, answers that are now being further refined by biologists studying tigers in India, Russia, and Southeast Asia. In Schaller's pioneering study, the tools used were fairly basic: binoculars, camera, scales, tape measure, and a notebook. His findings were greatly advanced by Seidensticker, Sunquist, and Smith, who added radio-telemetry to their tool kit. Biologists now employ additional tools like camera traps and global positioning systems, and the quest for more refined knowledge continues.

Wildlife managers usually act with the goal of maintaining or increasing animal populations. For example, they may suppress forest fires, manipulate vegetation or create water resources. However, ultimately they need to know how different wildlife species respond to these management measures. Therefore, monitoring populations or, put simply, counting animals periodically, is a vital part of wildlife biology. Wildlife scientists have long recognized that under most field situations it is impossible to get a total count of all animals in a population, for instance, all chital deer in a large forest reserve. Dense vegetation, extensive areas and the mobility of target species, all combine to make such total counts impractical.

What do biologists do in such a situation? Earlier, in Chapter 5, we saw how they count large, hoofed animals using distance sampling. Distance sampling is just one rigorous method among several used to count animals. In fact, most standard methods of wildlife science are rooted in the application of an old, well-tested tool from the statistician's kit: population sampling. By making individual measurements of parameters (for example, body size, sex ratio, population density) from a representative sample of animals drawn from a population, the statistician can make reliable inferences about an entire population—including unsampled individuals.

In fact, we routinely use sampling techniques in everyday life: such as to estimate the average nutritional intake of citizens, annual rate of inflation, readership of newspapers, voters' political preferences, or farmers' crop yields. No one would be foolish enough to go to every person in this vast country to answer such questions, because sampling methods give reliable enough answers, efficiently. This is true of questions in wildlife biology as well.

Identifying hair, bones and other remains of prey in representative samples of the scats (droppings) of carnivores help us understand their food habits. Herbivore diets can be determined by obtaining representative samples from their rumens. Properly sampled behavioural observations yield information on how animals budget their time, interact with each other and the kind of food they eat. Sample counts help in estimating proportions of different sexes and age classes in animal populations. Combined with periodic estimates of animal numbers, such demographic data enable wildlife biologists to understand animal population dynamics. Sampling methods permit scientists to measure how animals use different habitats, providing insights for managing them.

The greatest advantage of wildlife sampling-based methods is that they are quantitative and replicable by different observers. They are not dependent on the subjective opinions of individuals. Moreover, the parameters of interest (say, deer population density) estimated from such methods also generate measures of their uncertainty such as sampling variance and confidence intervals.

The last few decades have seen a veritable explosion of knowledge in wildlife population sampling methods. The cross-fertilization of ideas between wildlife biologists, statisticians, and computer programmers has led to refinements of many older field techniques. Because wildlife data are generated by complex and highly variable ecological 'systems' (as opposed to almost identical parts produced by a machine), the task of 'modelling nature' has become increasingly complex. Fortunately, as wildlife scientists honed their tools to tackle these complexities, the information technology revolution has made their work more tractable. Numerous, freely available wildlife software applications are now spurring the development of objective modern wildlife science from its original roots in subjective natural history. However, to benefit from the current revolution in wildlife science, field data must be collected under a regimen of sampling. Wildlife policy makers and managers in India have not yet woken up to this reality, leading to an acute manifestation of science deficiency in our conservation practices.

Saddled as they are with numerous day-to-day management problems that need urgent attention, Indian foresters scarcely have the room to understand or apply rigorous wildlife science. More often than not, they do not have the aptitude or technical training either. As a result, home-grown 'methods' such as 'waterhole census', 'block census', 'pugmark census' and suchlike have gained currency by default. Because these 'census' methods are based on the fundamental fallacy that all animals in a population can be counted over vast landscapes, they have neither theoretical nor empirical foundations.

The fallacy goes unchallenged, generating a mushroom cloud of official pseudo-data that enters the public domain without going through the scientific process of peer review and publication. As a result, reliable, scientifically proven methods that are simpler to apply are ignored. The ignorance about wildlife science (and of the scientific culture) in the popular media compounds the problem. The monitoring of our endangered national animal, the tiger, provides a brilliant case study of this phenomenon.

Thirty-five years ago, major efforts were launched worldwide to save tigers. Most Asian countries which had tigers passed laws to control hunting and established protected reserves. Implementing these laws was another matter, however. The burden fell on underpaid forest personnel who often did not possess the necessary resources, training or public support. Consequently, the tiger's overall decline continued, except in parts of India and Nepal, where most of the world's wild tigers survived. The pragmatic efforts of India's foresters, backed by political will at the highest levels and some public support, resulted in the establishment of several effective tiger reserves in the early 1970s. At least in these few pockets, tiger populations recovered (see Chapter 10).

However, the fact is that the official tiger numbers are at odds with what we know about tiger ecology today. A few examples: it is scientifically established that tigers attain higher population densities in prey-rich areas. Yet, the pugmark censuses show high tiger densities in prey-poor habitats like the mangrove swamps of the Sundarban; a major tiger reserve in the south reported a sudden leap in its tiger population from 54 to 66 a few years ago, and yet, absurdly, reported that only one of these animals was a cub. The same reserve had earlier reported annual population increases of 50–60 per cent among species such as deer, gaur and pigs, a biological impossibility. Many official censuses, conducted in daytime, routinely report counts of nocturnal animals like porcupines and mouse deer, sometimes even citing numbers of males and females! Despite a huge financial outlay and good intentions, the serious task of auditing tiger conservation has been turned into a farce.

How did this state of affairs come about? Through the 1970s and 1980s, Asia's reserve managers were ordered by their governments to count their tigers. Until then most forest managers in Asian countries had simply guessed at tiger numbers. Since the 1960s, Indian foresters have been making the claim that they can find and identify every individual tiger in this vast country simply by looking at paw prints (pugmarks) lifted from dusty trails. Confident assertions at official meetings, rather than scientific results, form the basis for claims of being able to census tigers not only in specific reserves, but over the entire country.

When forest managers continued to report dramatic country-wide increases in tiger numbers, year after year the IUCN (World Conservation Union) and other conservation agencies, eagerly awaiting a 'success story' were all too happy to hear them. Ignoring the warnings of tiger biologists, they blithely repeated the official tiger numbers, lending them credibility in the public eye. Relying on such numbers, a senior Indian official even asked in 1982 with rhetorical flourish: what do you do after you have succeeded in saving the tiger?

However, in the early 1990s when evidence of the numbing scale of tiger poaching for the bone trade emerged, this complacency was shattered. It became clear that the tiger numbers being trumpeted by various Asian governments were practically worthless. The reason was not far to seek: these figures were generated employing techniques that had never passed muster through peer review and publication, a process that is the touchstone of modern science.

In the absence of reliable population monitoring, there is no way of knowing whether efforts to save tigers are succeeding or failing. While the conservation community responds with increasing concern to the tiger's plight, there is an urgent need for wildlife managers to use more accurate methods to measure the effectiveness of their actions. These efforts are otherwise bound to flounder, much like a business enterprise that carries on without ever drawing up a balance sheet.

A key hurdle in appreciating the gravity of this problem in India is that most lay conservationists, and even biologists untrained in quantitative population ecology, believe the simple-minded notion that one can actually go out and count tigers and come up with a total number. Their elation and despondency is tied to the rise and fall in official tiger numbers. In fact, there is no need for either grief or joy based on these pugmark census results: these tiger numbers have no discernible relationship to real tiger numbers one way or the other.

The logical disconnect between real tiger numbers and the tally claimed from pugmark censuses arises because several key underlying assumptions of the 'pugmark census' are violated in practice. The fact that survey teams cannot search everywhere over hundreds of thousands of square kilometres of habitats, and that they cannot locate tracks of every tiger even where they reach, because of inappropriate soil conditions, both lead to undercounts.

On the other hand, not recognizing the variations in shape of the same paw-print, caused by soil type, slope and speed of movement of the animal, and the consequent recording of multiple prints of the same tiger as different animals, usually leads to over-counts. Further complicating the matter is the fact that the search effort put in, personnel employed and field conditions varies widely between different locations. As a cumulative consequence, the so-called tiger numbers derived from pugmark censuses have no consistent, predictable relationship with real tiger numbers.

Is there any alternative? Indeed there is. The fact that tiger numbers can be more reliably estimated using approaches based on population sampling rather than from censuses is not apparent to most people. However, the same people will readily accept that it is impossible to talk to every voter before predicting the results of an election or to visit every kitchen in the country to estimate levels of nutrition, or even to approach every consumer to assess the popularity of a brand of soap. Therefore, to get a reliable handle on voter preference, levels of nutrition, or the popularity of a soap brand, they accept results generated from sampling processes. When it comes to an even more difficult challenge, that of counting an

elusive animal like the tiger throughout our vast country, how can they believe otherwise?

Before getting into details, we need to step back and ask a simple question: with what degree of exactness do we really need to know tiger numbers? It quickly becomes apparent that for most conservation purposes on the enormous countrywide or regional scale there is no need to know exact tiger numbers. At this geographic scale, managers just need to know *where* the tiger populations are. This information is sufficient to track the extirpation of tiger populations or detect the establishment of new ones over time, for which we just need to systematically map the presence or absence of tigers: there is no need to count tigers at all. At the more tractable scale of individual tiger reserves, managers need to assess annually if their tiger populations are holding steady, going up, or going down. For the purpose of making management decisions and course corrections all that managers need is an index that is 'monotonically' linked to real tiger numbers (that is, when numbers go up the index goes up, when the numbers dwindle the index dips). A few critical tiger populations in important tiger reserves or in areas where biological studies are conducted demand the need for more accurate tiger numbers. Only in such cases do we need to really worry about estimating the exact tiger population size or densities.

These three levels of tiger monitoring will require increasingly sophisticated technical skills and equipment. The present tiger census approach has failed because it ignores the first two basic levels of tiger monitoring, and instead tries to achieve the most sophisticated level of monitoring across the entire country using absurdly simple-minded ideas.

How then can we visualize an alternative framework for monitoring wild tigers that is robustly scientific?

The sampling-based methods that I describe below explicitly recognize and deal with the problems associated with estimating two key parameters: the fraction of the total area that was surveyed, and the probability of finding tigers in the area surveyed. The pugmark census method, on the other hand, simply does not bother about this critical issue. It assumes, as a matter of 'faith', that both these proportions are equal to 100 per cent. Clearly, for secretive animals like tigers that are distributed over hundreds of square kilometres of rugged forested landscapes even in a single reserve, such naiveté cannot be the basis for reliable monitoring.

When mapping the countrywide distribution of tigers, sampling-based monitoring would simply involve a large number of survey personnel walking potential tiger trails, to record encounters with tiger signs. Tigers mark their passage by leaving tracks and depositing scats, their visiting cards for communicating with others of their species. By systematically surveying the presence of such signs to plot them on maps, using multiple-survey samples, observers can map the places where tigers occur as well as estimate the proportion of the total area tigers are likely to be present in, even if survey teams did not find tiger signs in many places. The statistical trick is to tease out the likelihood of tigers *not being present* from simply *not finding their signs* during the survey. Fortunately, in recent times ecologists and statisticians have developed some powerful techniques to deal with such 'presence versus non-detection' data.

At the next level of sophistication, managers only need a quantitative index that simply tells them if tiger numbers in a reserve are holding steady, going up or going down, without knowing how many animals there are. The average number of tiger track sets or scats encountered for every ten kilometres walked by survey teams can provide a simple index of how tiger populations have been faring

in a reserve over the years. I have successfully used forest department staff and naturalist-volunteers in several tiger reserves of Karnataka and Maharashtra to conduct such index surveys.

Another reliable indicator of potential tiger numbers is the density of their prey species. Scientific studies show that tiger densities are strongly correlated with the number of prey available in the form of wild and domestic ungulates. Because these cats kill roughly ten per cent of standing prey numbers every year, and an average tiger needs about fifty prey animals each year, prey numbers give us a rough estimate of possible tiger numbers. Prey numbers can be relatively easily derived using distance sampling (see Chapter 5).

All three methods suggested above require no advanced tools or highly trained personnel. However, they do require an initial survey design prepared by a competent scientist.

Only in a few priority conservation areas may there be a real need to actually estimate tiger numbers, either for research or to set management benchmarks. Currently the best scientific approach for estimating tiger densities is based on 'capture-recapture sampling'. This statistical concept was invented by the eighteenth-century French mathematician P.S. Laplace, and has been extensively developed by ecologists, statisticians, and computer programmers in recent years. It is based on the idea of repeatedly drawing samples of 'identifiable individual animals' from a population of which we want to estimate the size.

In this approach, biologists 'capture' sample animals from the target population and mark these individual animals using rings, bands, tags—whatever is practical—so that they can be identified, before releasing them. Subsequently some more samples of animals are caught from the population, each captured animal being given a unique identification and released. Scientists factor in how frequently the identified individuals are recaptured in complex computations to determine the average probability of catching an individual animal in the population. The estimated capture probability allows the biologist to estimate the total population size without the need to catch all individuals. As a simple example, if a biologist managed to catch and identify only twenty tigers in a survey, but based on their capture frequencies, the total proportion of animals caught was estimated as 50 per cent, the estimated total tiger population size, including uncaught tigers, is forty animals.

Estimating the numbers of animals like rats, fish and birds requires us to physically catch and mark individuals (hence the alternative name of this method: mark-recapture sampling). But the method works equally well for animals that can be individually identified using any other means. The fact that tigers (and leopards, jaguars, zebras, etc.) are identifiable based on their coat patterns hands us a great advantage. There is no need to catch and paint unique marks on tigers because, luckily for us, nature has done that job already! Therefore, photographs of tigers obtained using 'camera traps' hidden along forest trails can be used to sample tiger populations.

The camera trap I use consists of a flash-equipped, auto-focus camera wired to an electronic beam not unlike that in a burglar alarm. Every evening, I would go to the forest and set several traps across trails frequently used by tigers. While I slept peacefully at night, tigers would pad down the trail, break the beam, and take their own pictures. My results showed that tiger densities vary greatly, primarily depending on prey abundance. Densities range from a low of less than one or two tigers per 100 square kilometres in the prey-impoverished Sundarban mangrove forests to as high as eighteen tigers per 100 square kilometres in the grasslands of Kaziranga which are packed with ungulate prey. Densities in the famed tiger reserves of India, like Nagarahole and Kanha, fall in between, at about twelve tigers per 100 square kilometres.

It has been recently suggested that other kinds of individual identifications of tigers may be possible: DNA material from tiger scats, scent-based individual tiger identities made by trained police dogs or even individual identification of tiger paw-print shapes using statistical analyses. These are some of the possibilities being explored. However, these approaches have not yet been scientifically validated under field conditions, which is a prerequisite for using them within the powerful capture-recapture sampling framework described earlier. Some of these approaches, still being developed, may hold promise.

The science deficiency described above is not unique to monitoring tigers. It extends to almost every aspect of wildlife management in India. Most habitat manipulations now carried out by forest departments in our reserves are not based on prior testing of their varied consequences. The creation of waterholes, pre-burning or fire suppression, pulling out weeds, fertilizing bamboo and planting of trees, have all become a set of responses with scarcely any scientific justification, mainly pursued for spending massive budgetary allocations.

It is clear that while wildlife science is advancing rapidly, conservation practices in India have not kept pace. Several institutional and cultural changes are needed to address this deficiency. First, we have to throw out our naïve traditions of wildlife management and accept scientific methods. Second, the task of monitoring wildlife management should be taken away from untrained nature reserve managers who work under incredible day-to-day pressures. Third, involvement of qualified wildlife biologists in wildlife research, training, and monitoring programmes, must be encouraged rather than actively discouraged as at present. Fourth, there has to be a massive quantitative and qualitative increase in the genuine professional training of our wildlife managers.

In other fields of endeavour like agriculture, space exploration, manufacturing, medicine, communication, and information technology, India has benefited immensely from scientific advances during the last three decades. How much longer can this country afford the deeply rooted institutional lethargy that stunts the very possibility of scientific progress revolutionizing wildlife conservation?

12

Sacred Groves for the New Century

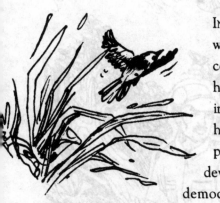

INDIAN SOCIETY HAS BEEN GRAPPLING with the contentious problem of conserving its wildlife for over a half century now, with a marked intensification of efforts in the second half of this period. India's massive population increase, rapid industrial development, and the rise in both democratic and material aspirations among people of all sections of society, have meanwhile weighted the balance heavily against wildlife. Yet despite all odds, India has managed to hang on, however precariously, to several assemblages of extinction-prone animals at least within the confines of its protected areas. When compared to the virtual elimination or large-scale range shrinkages among large animal faunas of Europe, North America and China during comparable periods of development, this is a remarkable achievement.

Half a century of conservation experience in India has thrown

up both successes and failures. India's success in holding on to threatened wildlife species—such as rhinos, elephants, and tigers— is quite spectacular when compared to the record of other Asian countries (with the possible exception of Nepal), which have undergone comparable social transitions. However, major failures have also marred this effort. The failure to scientifically manage wildlife, and the inflexibility of the Indian government in dealing with issues affecting local people, are two glaring examples.

We must examine the current challenges of wildlife conservation in India in the light of both empirical experience and conservation science. I would argue that for this debate to progress beyond the usual sterile polemics of 'wildlife versus people' or of 'state versus community management of wildlife', the terms 'wildlife' and 'conservation' have to be defined a little more rigorously.

'What is wildlife conservation?' may seem like a stupid question, when we consider the millions avidly watching television channels like *Discovery*, *National Geographic* and *Animal Planet*. However, such audience interest is not matched by an increased awareness of what truly constitutes wildlife conservation. To the average educated Indian, 'wildlife conservation' is synonymous with defence of animal rights or even with environmental advocacy or social activism. Such perceptions are seriously flawed: animal rights, environmentalism, and social activism are all concepts that are fundamentally distinct from wildlife conservation.

Advocates of animal rights value animals as *individuals*. For example, from a purely animal rights perspective, each one of India's eighteen billion or so domesticated animals—such as cattle, dogs and chickens—have exactly the same 'value' as an individual within the last surviving herd of brow-antlered deer of Manipur. On the other hand, wildlife conservationists would clearly value that deer inordinately more than cows and buffaloes, because of its 'rarity' and 'wildness'. They would overwhelmingly prioritize the 'right' of the deer species to survive, over the right of each individual cow or chicken.

Environmentalism is primarily concerned with the goal of making the world a better place for us human beings. Consequently, for environmentalists, wildlife conservation occupies only a narrow band within a wider spectrum of people-centric issues, such as urban air pollution or rural sanitation. Social activism is even further removed from wildlife conservation concerns, because the 'rights' of a single species, *Homo sapiens*, are central to its agenda.

Although wildlife conservation is often claimed as a goal by advocates of animal rights, environmentalism or social activism, this is usually for reasons of tactics or fashion, rather than serious concern about preserving the qualities of rarity and wildness that naturalists cherish. With few exceptions, most environmentalists and social activists are not 'naturalists': most would be bored to tears at the thought of sitting in a hide for days on end looking out for the elusive deer or tiger. I am not making value judgements here, merely pointing out that concern for preserving nature expressed by those who are not naturalists may not always be genuine.

Another term that often confounds discussion of wildlife conservation issues is 'biodiversity'. This is a scientific term that is being widely misapplied to mean all sorts of things, including human cultural diversity. The fact is that biodiversity includes all living creatures ranging from soil organisms to cultivated plants. Scientists measure it at the scale of genes, species, ecological communities, and landscapes. Quite a bit of the earth's biodiversity, including many plants (crops, for example) and animals (cows or rats for example), survives quite well on human-dominated landscapes like cities, farms,

and disturbed forests. A large part of this biodiversity can, and will, survive and proliferate without much effort on our part or even *because* of our avid pursuit of biotechnology.

Therefore, I will readily concede a point around which there is a surfeit of unnecessary polemics in India: is the goal of saving biodiversity compatible with human exploitation of animals or their habitats? Of course it is. Many forms of 'biodiversity' can and do coexist with such exploitation. Some forms of biodiversity may in fact be capable of surviving even higher pressures. These forms of biodiversity do not need inviolate sacred groves (of whatever size) to survive. Therefore, in this essay I focus on a smaller subset of biodiversity that I categorize as 'wildlife'. Thus defined, wildlife conservation becomes largely (but not exclusively) an issue of preserving viable populations, communities and habitats of free-ranging, extinction-prone, larger animals: for example, rhino, tiger, elephant, lion-tailed monkey, great hornbill, great Indian bustard, spotted eagle, king cobra, great white shark.

What are the traits of wildlife species that render them vulnerable to extinction? Two biological traits that we humans cannot alter through progressive legislation or social activism become immediately apparent: body size and diet. Larger body size is linked to greater dietary needs and hence to large home ranges and extensive movement. This is true even for herbivorous species such as elephants, whose food may be relatively abundant. When elephants move across landscapes, they are attracted to patches of protein-rich agricultural crops, even where natural forage is abundant. Where natural forage has been depleted through livestock grazing, bamboo extraction or forest fires, crop raiding by elephants becomes a severe problem.

A carnivorous diet further accentuates this wide-ranging

behaviour of large animals. We saw earlier that the size of a tiger's home range may extend from 15 to 500 square kilometres. A tigress raising cubs, who must kill sixty-seventy prey animals in a year, will kill any cattle she encounters on her forays simply because they are easier to kill than wild prey. If the wild prey is depleted, she will prey solely on cattle, and occasionally on humans.

Social-spacing behaviours such as territoriality, dispersal and seasonal migrations also lead to landscape-level animal movements. For ensuring their long-term survival (even using the more easily attained goal of 'demographic viability' rather than the more demanding criteria of 'genetic viability'), populations of such species require large landscapes free of incompatible human activities. Therefore, traditional conservation areas like sacred groves, much favoured by social activists, are simply not big enough to hold viable populations of creatures like tigers, elephants or rhinos. Nor can temple ponds sustain sea turtle populations. If such landscape and seascape creatures are to survive into the new century they need much larger 'sacred groves', which must be demarcated using strict biological criteria.

In India, the extirpation of the cheetah and the near extirpation of the wolf, and the shrinkage of breeding populations of tigers and lions to less than two per cent of their former range, demonstrates that 'coexistence' with humans has cost them dearly in the last few centuries. The elimination of elephants in the last century from extensive forest areas in the Western Ghats that are honeycombed with agricultural enclaves, shows that when conflicts ensue, the interests of humans will prevail.

Not all extinction-prone wildlife species are large, wide-ranging or carnivorous. Many are vulnerable simply because they occupy narrowly defined ecological niches. Some critical foods of the lion-

tailed macaques and great hornbills of the Western Ghats are available only in rainforest trees or lianas. They shelter only in old-growth tall timber. If these critical elements are dismantled through habitat exploitation, such species cannot survive.

Given all these problems why should we try to conserve wildlife? Surprisingly, both the utilitarian and ethical perspectives justify such conservation. The former emphasizes the value of wildlife for human use: as a source of genes or natural designs to keep our future options in biotechnology open; as a benchmark to assess the degree of deleterious modifications of the environment; as a recreational, educational or aesthetic resource for us in an increasingly artificial world; as an integral component of landscapes that protect our soil and water; or even as a source of products for our 'wise use' and 'sustainable consumption'.

On the other hand, from an ethical perspective, it can be argued that the present generation does not own wildlife but only holds it in trust for future generations. Or even that species that evolved before humans should have a right to continue the process of their natural evolution.

Whatever the justification, the current global consensus cutting across ideological barriers, is that wildlife needs to be conserved. The ongoing debates and discord around wildlife conservation centre on *how*, rather than *why* wildlife should be conserved. The Indian experience in conservation, stretching over a century, can contribute significantly to the resolution of these debates at the global level, and needs a closer look.

As historian Mahesh Rangarajan has documented, the 1970s saw the emergence of a predominantly preservationist, top-down paradigm of wildlife conservation in India. The policy focused on setting up protected areas, establishing anti-poaching measures, curbing forest exploitation and placing restrictions on activities such as livestock grazing, arson, and collection of non-timber forest products. In some cases to reduce human impacts on wildlife, villages were relocated out of wildlife reserves, although not always in a fair or sensitive manner.

The ecological consequences of these measures were fairly dramatic: in many parks such as Kanha, Ranthambhore, and Nagarahole, shot-over and degraded habitats recovered and wildlife populations rebounded to levels unseen since the eighteenth century. Unfortunately, because of institutional weaknesses in the forest departments (see Chapter 11), this dramatic recovery process was not scientifically documented. Indian foresters, who did quite a remarkable job of recovering wildlife in these reserves, were not trained to apply the necessary science. Neither did they permit others who could, to do so, because they perceived these reserves as their fiefdoms. The cause-and-effect relationship between the preservationist measures taken and the wildlife recoveries was not demonstrated to the conservation community at large. This is particularly true of the generation of conservationists who, taking charge after the first decade of recovery, had not witnessed dismal state of affairs in the 1950s and 1960s (see Chapters 2–3, and 10).

During the 1980s, as environmentalism and conservation became mainstream ideologies globally, the first generation of biocentric naturalists and preservationists that had headed international conservation agencies was replaced by a new and savvy breed of conservation executives schooled in social sciences, business management, and law. Possessing neither a theoretical understanding of ecology nor practical experience in wildlife conservation, this new crop of conservation leaders saw wildlife reserves that restricted human activities as unnecessarily harsh, anti-

people anachronisms. The new manifestoes of conservation they generated, beginning with *The World Conservation Strategy* of 1982 and culminating in *Caring for the Earth*, underplayed the importance of protected areas in saving wildlife (although some lip service was paid to such areas.) The newly fashioned paradigm of 'sustainable use' argued that protected areas that restricted resource use—particularly by 'local communities'—were not important. The proponents of these ideologies delicately danced around the hard issue of whether the use of force to protect wildlife was justifiable. Instead they advocated 'wise use' of nature reserves by 'local people', arguing that this would automatically make people protect wildlife and the need for tough law enforcement would wither away.

This model of painless wildlife conservation became instantly popular with everyone in the conservation business. Leading ecologists like Madhav Gadgil embraced it, arguing that conservation had to move beyond preserving large animals in protected reserves, and take into account 'people' in the landscapes beyond. Governments and protected area managers too loved the new thrust, because it relieved them of the thankless and unpleasant duty of protecting wildlife through the use of force.

Social and human rights activists liked the new model even more: If conservationists themselves said strict protected areas were unnecessary, why should they, whose primary concern was the people's rights to resources, object? The sustainable use ideology sounded most attractive to representatives of local people whose hunger for land and biomass locked up in the wildlife reserves was growing exponentially because of population growth, breakdown of traditions, and rising aspirations.

The term 'sustainable use' and its cousin 'sustainable development' soon percolated from the developmental arena into the

conservation field. Buzzwords like 'Community-based Conservation', 'Integrated Conservation and Development' and 'Eco-development' became fashionable in the lexicons of conservationists, environmentalists, and social activists. By the mid-1990s even India's notoriously dogmatic foresters had picked up the new lingo—many among them clearly spotting a gravy train loaded with lucrative international aid projects, foreign trips, and consultancies.

This blurring of the distinction between 'conservation', 'development', and 'human welfare' was articulated in *Caring for the Earth*, published jointly by the IUCN, World Wide Fund for Nature (WWF) and the United Nations Environment Program (UNEP). In an insightful critique called *Limits to Caring*, published in 1993, ecologist John Robinson pointed out the fatal flaw in the new conservation mantra. Robinson argued that while sustainable use was indeed *one* powerful approach to conservation under *some* circumstances, it was not a universally applicable model that eliminated the need for effective protected areas that kept out incompatible human impact.

Robinson argued that because conservation has to scientifically balance the size and productivity of biological resources against the numbers of consumers, in many cases, the new paradigm could neither sustain supplies of goods and services from protected areas to the people, nor could it lead to viable conservation. Instead, Robinson advocated the alternative paradigm of 'sustainable landscapes'. His strategy, described by *International Wildlife* as 'carving up tomorrow's world', suggested maintaining a mix of strictly protected areas for preserving sensitive wildlife species and ecosystems, multiple-use conservation areas for perpetuating a larger subset of biodiversity tolerant of human impacts, and intensive use of other agricultural and industrial landscapes to primarily meet human needs.

The implications of Robinson's critique of user-friendly conservation models were serious, but largely ignored by the conservation community. However, they have been abundantly borne out by events of the subsequent decade.

The cumulative effect on wildlife of the 'sustainable use' paradigm shift has been disastrous in India. Even as demographic and social pressures on the nature reserves have mounted, and international trade and commerce in endangered species boomed, official wildlife protection mechanisms have gone into serious neglect and decline. By the late 1990s, India's wildlife reserves had perhaps lost about 60 per cent of the protective capabilities that existed a decade earlier. Although numerous social factors have contributed to this decline, the seductive siren song of 'eco-development' was the most critical element.

Gradually, biologists who were largely preoccupied during the preceding two decades with their own narrowly focused 'backpack and binoculars' field studies, or with fashionable ecological theories that emerged like characters in search of a play, began waking up to the fact that widespread misapplication of the sustainable use paradigm by governments, international development agencies and even conservation agencies, was leading to serious erosion of wildlife and wild lands. They began to focus instead on rigorous studies of the impacts of human use and disturbance on wildlife and habitats resulting in a series of recent syntheses (see 'Further Reading'). These studies show that if the current wildlife decline is to be reversed, conservationists have to move beyond politically correct buzzwords and build workable conservation models based on hard ecological and socio-economic data. The implications of these new studies

deserve serious consideration in the Indian context, where wildlife conservation has to address two major challenges: illegal hunting and degradation of wildlife habitats.

Hunting assumes several forms in India. Poaching caters not only to the hunger for meat, the needs of organized illegal trade suck in high-value products such as tiger bone, rhino horn, elephant ivory, bear gall-bladder, and shatoosh wool. Undercover investigations have revealed widespread trafficking. This lucrative commerce has driven many species of birds, mammals, and reptiles to the verge of extinction. Even the most distant village is now effectively networked to wildlife trade in urban centres. The remotest forest communities of India now aspire to quick profits through such trade. While I was studying tigers in Madhya Pradesh in 1995, petty traders on bicycles were distributing lethal insecticides to local villagers, encouraging them to poison tiger kills that they found while collecting tendu leaves or grazing cattle.

In a more recent study, my colleague Madhusudan and I documented over twenty different hunting techniques used by local people around the Nagarahole and Kudremukh reserves in Karnataka. These range from country-made firearms to a variety of traditional techniques that target very precisely the vulnerability of particular animal species. Giant squirrels, flying squirrels, monitor lizards, and even monkeys, are hunted with bows that shoot projectiles of hardened clay. Deer and wild pigs, and occasionally leopards, are choked to death in wire snares concealed across their paths. Monkeys, mouse deer, and hares are chased with dogs, netted and clubbed to death. Species that rest in tree cavities, such as palm civets, hornbills and other birds, are pulled out and killed by experts who can climb giant forest trees using nothing more than simple notches hacked on boles. Pangolins, porcupines, and monitor lizards are smoked out of their underground burrows and bludgeoned. Our study showed that densities of species favoured by poachers—such as chital, wild pig, langur and giant squirrels—were 80 per cent lower in poorly protected forests than in strictly protected zones.

Summarizing the findings from a recent world-wide study of wildlife hunting, ecologists John Robinson and Elizabeth Bennett conclude that most local hunting in tropical forest areas, either for the pot or for markets, is unsustainable because it is occurring at intensities way above the productivity of the targeted animal populations. Consequently, hunting is driving the decline and extirpation of many animal species, resulting in what conservationist Kent Redford aptly termed 'the empty forests'.

A dramatic example of a forest in the process of being so emptied right before our eyes is the Namdapha tiger reserve of Arunachal Pradesh: an inaccessible tract of glorious rainforest spread over 3000 square kilometres on the Indo-Myanmar border. While the forests of Namdapha look impressive, they are overrun with hunters from several local tribal groups. Snares and booby traps of all kinds await animal victims at every turn on the forest trails. Hunters armed with guns and poison arrows stalk and kill any large animal that moves. Ungulates like sambar, wild pig, muntjac, and takin are already scarce, as are their major predators like tigers and leopards.

These deadly traditional skills of forest people are now being put at the service of the international wildlife trade for a few hundred rupees or even a bottle of country-made liquor. Conservationists who plead for the coexistence of such traditional cultures inside wildlife conservation areas fail to perceive the lethal, synergistic impact that these ancient skills, current technologies and modern commerce has on wildlife.

Most of these empty forests show up as impressive swathes of green cover in the remotely sensed maps produced by the Indian space agency or the World Conservation Monitoring Centre in the UK. Unfortunately cameras mounted on satellites simply cannot penetrate forest canopies to track the faunal impoverishment underneath. Therefore, much of the debate around the extent of forest cover in India has little relevance to monitoring the fate of wildlife in these forests.

When hunting depresses animal densities below the natural carrying capacity of a habitat, animals stop playing their functional roles in the biological community. Poaching of animals and birds affects the plant community because these animals may disperse pollen and seeds of plants or consume their insect pests. Mega-herbivores such as elephants, rhinos, and wild cattle even modify the vegetation structure, thereby facilitating access of other animals to plant resources. Such ecological linkages are exceedingly complex, and as yet poorly understood. The changes induced by the hunting of one species may occur slowly, but they are inexorable, eliminating several co-evolved animals and plants, and affecting the plant community composition imperceptibly over time. Ecologists John Terborgh and Joel Berger have produced convincing evidence that such cascading effects can have major consequences for the long-term structure and functioning of animal and plant communities.

Apart from direct hunting, the second major factor underlying the decline of wildlife in India is the loss or degradation of habitat. A typical example of critical habitat loss is the natural grasslands in the deltas of the Ganga and Brahmaputra rivers. These once extensive Terai grasslands were home to an impressive assemblage of hoofed animals that included the elephant, Indian and Javan rhinos, wild buffalo, gaur, sambar, barasingha, brow-antlered deer, chital, hog deer, muntjac, wild pig, and the pygmy hog. These grasslands now occur only as tattered patches in reserves like Corbett, Chitwan, Manas, and Kaziranga. Except for Kaziranga, all the other patches have already lost several species. More than 99 per cent of this unique grassland habitat has simply been colonized by farmers and turned into productive farms. Although, as often pointed out by environmentalists, large developmental projects have played a role in loss of wildlife habitats, overall, the expansion of agriculture has been the overwhelmingly dominant force in driving habitat loss.

The threat of habitat degradation arises when contiguous habitats are fragmented by intrusion of human settlements, roads, railways, or pipelines. Such linear barriers may obstruct natural movements or gene flow in animal populations, affecting their long-term viability. Fragmentation increases the interface between habitat types, creating 'edge effects' that have different consequences for different species: animals that thrive in 'ecotones' fare better, whereas the ones that prefer deep interiors suffer. Consequently, fragmentation commonly benefits generalist species like crows or bonnet monkeys—derogatorily termed 'trash species' by conservationists—at the expense of rare species like the great hornbill or the lion-tailed macaque that occupy specialized niches. Risks of invasion by exotic alien plants and animals, or of the diseases spread by domestic animals, increase with advancing habitat fragmentation.

Whether wildlife habitats are fragmented or intact, changes in habitat 'quality' also greatly influence the population densities of animals. Sometimes, human impacts on habitat quality are obvious: an area overgrazed by livestock may support lower densities of wild ungulates than an area without cattle; a forest that is heavily logged for timber may be an inferior habitat for rainforest primates. In other cases, such effects are less obvious. The long-term consequences of the exploitation of non-timber forest products like fruits, leaves, bark, root, gum, resin, rattan, and bamboo can be particularly insidious. Often such harvests literally kill the forest: debarking of cinnamon or *Machilus* trees for manufacturing incense sticks, breaking branches of tendu trees to harvest leaves or of *Garcinias* to collect fruits, eventually kill these trees. Collection of amla fruits for making pickles or sal seeds for manufacturing cooking fat are likely to have genetic and demographic consequences for these plants. The impact of human disturbances on wildlife habitats is often cumulative. It is no surprise that the great pied hornbill is now a scarce bird in the rainforests of the Western Ghats: logging of giant softwood trees has eliminated its nesting cavities; collection of *Myristica* and other fruits has reduced its food supplies and its natural adaptation of sealing in the nesting females and chicks in tree cavities has made it an easy prey for hunters. Yet such non-timber forest product collection is often blindly touted as a 'conservation solution' by many conservationists.

There is no real evidence that the ecology of many endangered wildlife species, communities, and habitats can biologically adapt to cope with such market-driven impacts. While it is true that some levels of disturbance have existed in nature, and sometimes human activities formed a part of such disturbance regimes, there are no data to argue that all human-induced disturbances, at all intensities, regardless of origin, are beneficial to wildlife.

We cannot assume, just because the Masai herders in Africa 'co-exist' with large carnivores in landscapes over several thousand square kilometres, that human–predator coexistence is a feasible option in Indian wildlife reserves a few hundred square kilometres in size. We cannot ignore the fact that Masai reduce livestock losses to predators to tolerable levels by hunting predators. While the poor quality land on which Masai graze their cattle has few alternative uses, the productive forests of India offer temptingly profitable alternatives to sustaining either wildlife or rural herders. We also need to note that in the African context, such multiple-use areas exist outside of, and in addition to, large and strictly protected nature reserves. Often such protected areas are sources for surplus animals that are harvested outside.

The Maldhari herders of Gir are sometimes cited as coexisting harmoniously with lions because they traditionally tolerate livestock losses to lions. Yet, with the relocation of such herders from parts of Gir, the abundance of wild ungulates and their contribution to lion diet have both increased. The earlier simple predator–prey system comprising lions and domesticated buffaloes has now turned into a more 'natural' multiple prey–predator system. I would argue that maintaining this natural ecological integrity should be the goal of wildlife conservation in a context where functional lion-and-natural prey communities occupy less than a tenth of a per cent of their former distributional range.

The fact that India's villagers or adivasis are commonly hired as cheap labour to exploit forest products that supply distant markets is mistaken by many conservationists to be ecologically sensible, traditionally wise, 'harmonious coexistence' between conservation and local use of forests. There is no doubt that addressing the cash income needs that drive the rural poor in India to the wage labour involved in collecting forest products is a most urgent issue. However, this must be faced as an economic and social issue, without confusing ecological impacts and livelihood-related concerns. If social pressures compel us to carry on such practices, we should at least be honest about it and not pretend that we are promoting conservation.

It is clear that meeting the resource needs of our burgeoning human population must lie in the wise use of landscapes outside our legally designated wildlife reserves. Delinking these reserves from exploitative commerce, while providing adequate livelihood opportunities to people beyond their boundaries, holds the key to sustainable conservation. Those who decry arguments in favour of protected nature reserves as just a manifestation of whimsical authoritarianism on the part of socially insensitive green missionaries are clearly prioritizing rhetoric over reason.

To flip the reverse side of a question raised by ecologist Madhav Gadgil a few years ago, we must now practise conservation not only as if *people mattered*, but also as if *wildlife mattered*.

After years of sterile polemics, a dialogue about these issues now seems to be getting under way between champions of wildlife conservation and advocates of human interests. It is not going to be easy to find workable solutions because the conflict between wildlife and people is real. Outside of seminar halls, these conflicts cannot be swept away by a blizzard of politically correct buzzwords. The different 'stakeholders' (to use one such buzzword favoured by the World Bank) perceive the same wildlife reserve differently, and advance their own claims on it. Mediation among them may generate lasting solutions only if they are rooted in ecological knowledge.

Conservation options are, however, in the final analysis, political options. Solid scientific, moral, aesthetic, and pragmatic arguments can demonstrate that sacrificing the remaining land area earmarked for wildlife is unlikely to make any dent on the numerous human problems that we have been unable to resolve through deploying the land already earmarked for human use. The vast majority of local communities in India (urban, semi-urban and rural) have no access to resources inside protected areas. This will continue to be so in the future. Sacrificing the surviving wildlife reserves will not alter this big picture.

In an ideal world, the centralized state and its regulatory arms would ultimately wither away and all social policing functions would be replaced by voluntary changes in human behaviour. However, at this point in our history, the use of force to protect wildlife has to be acknowledged as a fundamental need. How best we can minimize this need and how it can be combined with the practice of participatory democracy are still evolving issues. In extreme situations, like that in the Kaziranga reserve of Assam which is under immense threat from hardened rhino poachers, a force of two hundred armed men patrolling continually provides effective protection. This conservation model would not work in the North-eastern hill states. Whether wildlife protection works better under a local authority or a more remote source of political power is an issue that needs to be explored in site-specific contexts. Given the huge diversity of social contexts in which conservation takes place in India, there may be as many answers as locations.

Conservationists must now use all their persuasive skills to educate the rest of society about these key wildlife conservation issues. At the same time they must actively try to implement workable conservation solutions in specific local contexts. There is no silver bullet, I am afraid, and there will never be a 'closure' in the wildlife conservation business. Yet, there is some room for hope, as the next essay illustrates.

13
Nagarahole: Shop or Shrine?

INDIA IS ONE-THIRD THE SIZE OF THE CONTINENTAL US, but supports about four times more people. Most of these people are poor, live off the land in some manner, use wood for fuel, and are unlettered. About one-fifth of the world's cattle occur in India although the country occupies less than 5 per cent of the earth's land surface. Set within this matrix of shrinking natural landscapes and widespread poverty, there is an urbanized middle class approximately the size of the population of France. The economy is growing at the rate of 7 per cent per year. If we can find conservation solutions here, we can probably find them anywhere.

Over centuries, as agriculture expanded and commerce and development proceeded apace, the forest frontier has continuously receded. The patches of forest that remain are now mostly within government-owned tracts known as reserved forests. The British

colonialists established these reserves nearly a hundred and fifty years ago, primarily for extracting timber and firewood; indirectly this curbed the expansion of the farming frontier that was pushing back the forests.

There is very little elbow room now left for fresh experiments to solve the problems of wildlife conservation that we examined earlier in this book. In this essay, we look at these general problems in the specific context of Nagarahole, a nature reserve in south-western India where I have worked for the past three decades.

The forests of Nagarahole are rich in many kinds of biodiversity, but are particularly well known for their valuable timber and charismatic animals like tigers and elephants. I first visited Nagarahole as an amateur naturalist in the 1960s, then returned to its boundaries as a farmer for a decade in the 1970s. Finally changing hats once again, over the last two decades, I have studied this area as a wildlife biologist. I hope I bring more than a purely academic perspective into this essay.

Nagarahole has been used as an extractive reserve for a long time by a variety of interests. Perhaps thousands of years ago, its hunter-gatherer communities lived at low densities, purely off the land. As population densities increased, the people took up slash-and-burn agriculture. Meanwhile, the farming frontier outside was also expanding and forests were shrinking, reducing slash-and-burn cycles.

In the 1860s, slash-and-burn farming was banned by the colonial government and Nagarahole was declared a reserved forest: a source of timber, firewood, and pasture for village cattle. The wood from the forest was used in nearby cities and towns for construction, or in the villages for agricultural implements and housing. The area was not only logged, but also extensively burned every year to improve livestock grazing and to promote the collection of a host

of forest products. A wide variety of these non-timber forest products, such as tree bark, fruits, roots, leaves, lianas and animal products, were intensively exploited to meet the growing demands of industrial and urban consumers.

In the 1950s, with all these pressures on the forest, there was very little wildlife left. There was serious conflict between wild animals such as tigers, leopards and elephants on the one hand, and local agricultural communities on the other. After the 1950s–60s, wider availability of shotguns and agricultural pesticides (used to poison predators) led to the virtual elimination of predators from the park. Added to this, commercial ivory hunting of elephants also began.

Tribal people with a very strong hunting culture inhabited the Nagarahole area. Outside the park, there were landed castes such as Kodava and Vokkaliga, who also took pride in hunting. The government had instituted a scheme for bounty hunting of tigers, leopards, and dholes in the area. A local friend of mine, who died recently, had shot twenty-eight tigers between 1948 and 1965, for a bounty of a hundred rupees for every tiger he shot. He did not even have to go far from his village near Nagarahole to do so: tigers came to the village, because that's where the cattle were.

In addition, there were other kinds of hunters. The tribal people employed a variety of ingenious native techniques to hunt. Snaring was a common technique as were a dozen other methods. Initially the snare hunters used natural fibres, but later they switched to steel wires. When I visited Nagarahole in the 1960s as a student, it was a park only on paper, and there did not appear to be much hope of its wildlife surviving.

However, by the early 1970s, there was a new social chemistry operating in India. One charismatic political leader, Mrs Indira

Gandhi, was personally a strong wildlife preservationist. There was also a growing middle-class lobby of conservationists who liked to watch animals, and who strongly pushed for the establishment of wildlife reserves. Finally, there was also a forest department, with a structure somewhat like the military, which was capable of serious law enforcement. This particular mix led to the establishment of the Nagarahole National Park (among others) and stricter enforcement generally of wildlife protection laws.

The objective of these efforts was wildlife preservation, and one of the major targets for enforcement was elimination of illegal hunting. Hunting prevailed on a wide scale because of patches of cultivation that existed inside the park. This cultivation attracted wild animals, and the animals attracted poachers. They entered the park, stayed with the cultivators, and hunted. Once the patrols started operating and hunting was made illegal, cultivation inside the park became virtually impossible because of increased animal damage to crops. Most cultivators were forced to move out with their livestock. After the 1970s, the crackdown on illegal hunting led to the abandonment of several settlements and to a dramatic increase in large mammal densities.

Another factor was the emergence of conservation awareness in India, about the damage that the forest department itself was inflicting on the forests through heavy logging and collection of forest products. A vocal lobby of conservationists succeeded in pressurizing the government to eliminate successively, clear-cutting, selective-cutting, and then all forms of forest product collection, in the two decades after 1974.

This process gradually led to a recovery of the wildlife populations. By the 1980s, Nagarahole had become a rich area for large mammals.

These animals are the most difficult to protect because they come into conflict with humans by destroying crops and livestock. Their meat, hide, bones, antlers or ivory are of great market value for poachers.

Nagarahole has three major large carnivores: tiger, leopard, and dhole. It is probably one of the prime areas in Asia where all three species exist at high densities. Dhole live in packs, and a pack has to kill a small deer-sized animal roughly every day. A single leopard has to make such a kill every ten days or so, and a tiger once a week. As long as the park had cultivation and cattle, and there was continual conflict between predators and livestock owners, the predators had little chance. Once the conflict was reduced and wild prey populations recovered, predator populations bounced back too.

This was the situation in 1986, when I returned to the area as a scientist. I was now documenting this recovery process with greater scientific rigour, because it was clear to me that we needed to understand how these large mammal communities functioned. In the long run, if they are to be saved, we must have the hard data on their ecological needs. We humans readily understand the needs of various other human stakeholders. But if conservation strategies are built without understanding the needs of wild animals, then they inevitably lose out.

So the focus of my study was to understand the ecological needs of this large mammal community in Nagarahole, composed of large herbivores and large predators. The first step was to use some very rigorous methods to estimate population densities of herbivores. It was then generally thought that tropical forests were poor areas for large herbivores, but this turned out to be untrue of Nagarahole.

I determined that the densities and biomass of herbivorous

mammals in Nagarahole were comparable to some of the best East African savannah areas. Densities of over sixty hoofed animals per square kilometre, added up to a live animal biomass—or total weight of live prey—of 15,000 kilograms per square kilometre.

I then moved on to study the predators. We often hear the argument that one could have predators and people both hunting off the same prey base. So I had to look very carefully at what the predators ate and how much they consumed. This involved studying their droppings and examination of their kills. These predation studies showed that the three predators in Nagarahole were taking most of the croppable surplus in many species: they were almost playing a regulatory role. There was clearly no room for one more major predator species in this system: particularly if that predator then went out selling the meat in nearby markets.

The next step was to understand the predator's needs of space. This involved putting radio-collars on tigers and leopards and tracking their movements. One breeding female tiger had a home range of about fifteen square kilometres. I also counted tigers using a new technique called camera-trap photography, where tigers took their own pictures and individual tigers could be identified by their stripes. This technique enabled me to accurately estimate the numbers of these secretive predators and understand their long-term population dynamics. I now have a pretty good idea of what it takes to support these tiger populations. A population with about twenty-five breeding females has a good chance of surviving in the long run. But if the number of breeding females drops down to five or six, as it had probably happened in 1967, the population would vanish soon.

My colleague Madhusudan and I made another major discovery when we looked at animal densities in the less protected forests of the region. We found enormous differences in densities. The wild ungulate and primate populations had dwindled sharply with the lack of strict protection in these areas.

Our survey also showed that the illegal hunters' haul of animals was not enough to make any significant impact on the local economy. From a purely economic point of view it did not matter much whether they hunted or not. Most hunting was done either for luxury consumption of wild proteins or to earn some petty cash. It was not hunting for livelihood in any sense of the word.

There are about 600,000 people living in the region around Nagarahole, who can be described as the 'local community'. Even within an area merely ten kilometres from the park boundary, the human population probably exceeds 120,000, or over 200 persons for every square kilometre of the park area. The option of 'sustainably' harvesting plant and animal products from Nagarahole, for 'equitable' sharing among all these 'local people' appears to be an impossible task. That attempts to do so would destroy the biological integrity of Nagarahole, and eliminate its fragile large mammal communities, is almost certain.

'Sustainability' in this context should mean sustaining whole biological systems including intact pieces of wild lands like Nagarahole. It should not be defined as sustaining the continuous supply of a few products, while the biological system itself gets impoverished. The moment even the most innocuous-looking resource extraction is linked to the global market, it can potentially have a devastating effect on the forest and wildlife. Some products, such as tiger bones, have huge international markets now. Therefore, market-driven solutions may not work for all species. We need to isolate some species and ecosystems from market pressures—if we want to conserve them.

The key players who influence the conservation business in Nagarahole include poor people who enter the forest to earn cash incomes through wage labour, local farmers and planters who employ them, the forest department bureaucracy which runs the park, and the vocal urban middle class, which contains both the social activists who promote human interests and conservationists who promote wildlife interests. A process of negotiation is now under way between these players to solve the problems that have been thrown up by the creation of the park thirty years ago. One approach that seems to hold promise is to keep animals and people separated at the scale of the park itself but promote coexistence at the larger landscape scale.

For example, the forest department has kept elephants away from farmland by digging trenches. These trenches, which keep elephants in the forest, also keep livestock out, thereby helping the forest regenerate. For the tribal people living inside the park, who demanded agricultural land and other social amenities, a voluntary resettlement scheme is under way.

When we look at the problems in Nagarahole, it is clear that long-term solutions lie in the wise use of landscapes outside. Delinking Nagarahole from rapidly globalizing markets and providing alternative livelihood opportunities for people who depend on its forests now, hold the key to the survival of the reserve in the long run.

It is not going to be easy to find practical solutions: the conflicts are real, and cannot be wished away. Everybody perceives Nagarahole in a different way. Different stakeholders are coming forward with their claims. The resulting negotiations may generate lasting solutions only if they do not ignore ecological and social realities.

Our collective moral dilemma boils down to whether Nagarahole should be treated as a shop or a shrine in our global village. In the light of this case study, I would like to re-emphasize the points I have made in my earlier essays. First, the widely popular model of 'biodiversity conservation through sustainable use' is not applicable to ecological and social contexts such as that of Nagarahole in southern Asia, if our definition of 'biodiversity' includes endangered large mammals. Second, linking the exploitation of biodiversity to global markets in order to create economic incentives for local stakeholders—a frequently touted conservation solution—will certainly lead to the elimination of several fragile forms of biodiversity. Third, instead of promoting 'sustainable use everywhere' *as the only conservation solution*, we should instead look at the alternative model of using overall landscapes in a sustainable manner, without sacrificing the ecological integrity of our nature reserves.

Throughout the course of human historical development we have often made the wrong choice, thereby destroying much of the splendid natural world we inherited. Many conservationists now believe that it is only a matter of time before the remaining wildlife and wild lands are swept away in a tidal wave of consumerist greed, pig-headed development and sheer human needs.

I am also certain that we will make many more such wrong social choices in the future, and lose some—perhaps quite a bit—of whatever wild nature remains. However, predicting our ecological future is a tricky business. If someone had asked me in the early 1960s whether any wildlife could survive in India until the turn of the century, my answer would have been a definite no. However, by the mid-1990s when the 'tiger crisis' made world headlines and most conservationists—and the BBC and *Time* magazine—predicted the imminent extinction of wild tigers, I had to strongly disagree. I did so based on the understanding I had gained in the intervening years. This understanding gives me reason for hope: a sense of cautious optimism that wild tigers, rhinos, and elephants will continue to roam freely somewhere on this fragile planet well into the next century and beyond. How many such places will remain on this earth is a question that only our generation has the power to decide.

Further Reading

Anderson, K. 2002. *Kenneth Anderson Omnibus* (Volumes 1–2). Rupa & Co., New Delhi

Dinerstein, E. 2003. *The return of the unicorns*. Columbia University Press, New York.

Karanth, K.U. 2001. *The way of the tiger: Natural history and conservation of the endangered big cat*. Colin Baxter Photography, UK and Centre for Wildlife Studies, Bangalore.

_____, and J.D. Nichols, (Editors). 2002. *Monitoring tigers and their prey: A manual for researchers, managers and conservationists in tropical Asia*. Centre for Wildlife Studies, Bangalore, India.

_____, J.D. Nichols, J. Seidensticker, E. Dinerstein, J.L.D. Smith, C. McDougal, A.J.T. Johnsingh, R.S. Chundawat and V. Thapar. 2003. Science deficiency in conservation practice: The monitoring of tiger populations in India. *Animal Conservation* 6: 141–6.

_____, J.D. Nichols, N.S. Kumar, W.A. Link and J.E. Hines. 2004. Tigers and their prey: Predicting carnivore densities from prey abundance. *Proceedings of the National Academy of Sciences, USA* 101(14): 4854–8.

Kramer, R., C. van Schaik, and J. Johnson. 1997. *Last stand: Protected areas and the defense of tropical biodiversity.* Oxford University Press, New York.

Levin, S. 1999. *Fragile dominion: Complexity and the commons.* Persus Publishing, Cambridge, USA.

Madhusudan, M.D. and K.U. Karanth. 2002. Local hunting and the conservation of large mammals in India. *Ambio* 31: 49–54.

Rangarajan, M. 2001. *India's wildlife history.* Permanent Black, New Delhi.

Redford, K.H. 1992. The empty forest. *Bioscience* 42: 412–22

Robinson, J.G. 1993. Limits to caring: Sustainable living and the loss of biodiversity. *Conservation Biology* 7: 8–20.

_____, and E.L. Bennet. 2000. *Hunting for sustainability in tropical forests.* Columbia University Press, New York.

Schaller, G.B. 1967. *The deer and the tiger.* University of Chicago Press, Chicago.

Seidensticker, J., S. Christie, and P. Jackson (Editors). 1999. *Riding the tiger: Tiger conservation in human dominated landscapes.* Cambridge University Press, Cambridge.

Soule, M.E. and G. Lease. 1995. *Reinventing nature? Response to postmodern deconstruction.* Island Press, Washington, DC.

Sunquist, F. and M.E. Sunquist. 1988. *Tiger moon.* University of Chicago Press, Chicago.

Terborgh, J. 1999. *Requiem for nature*. Island Press, Washington, DC.

____, C. van Schaik, L. Davenport, and M. Rao. 2002. *Making parks work: Strategies for preserving tropical nature*. Island Press, Washington, DC.

Treves, A. and K.U. Karanth. 2003. Human–Carnivore conflict and perspectives on carnivore management worldwide. *Conservation Biology* 17(6): 1491–9.